Interpreting
the Gospel
of John

Gary M. Burge

BAKER BOOK HOUSE
Grand Rapids, Michigan 49516

©1992 by
Baker Book House Company
Box 6287
Grand Rapids, Michigan 49516–6287.
All rights reserved

Printed in the United States of America

Library of Congress Cataloging-in-Publication Data

Burge, Gary M., 1952–
   Interpreting the Gospel of John/ Gary M. Burge.
      p.   cm.   — (Guides to New Testament Exegesis ; 5)
   Includes bibliographical references.
   ISBN 0-8010-1021-7
   1. Bible. N.T. John—Criticism, interpretation, etc. I. Title. II. Series.
   II. Series.
   BS2615.2.B87   1992
   226.5'061—dc20   91-43448

To Kenneth E. Bailey

Teacher, Friend, and Colleague
whose lectures in Beirut in 1973
inspired my commitment
to the New Testament
and the people of the Middle East.

Contents

Introduction

The Gospel of John unceasingly inspires and fascinates students and scholars. Each year hundreds of journal articles and books contribute to the accumulation of interpretative thought. At first reading John's message seems simple and straightforward, yet its simplicity is deceptive. The number of Johannine interpretative riddles are legion. Even if we agree on the meaning of the text, we must explain how this literature fits into the history of the early church. Who wrote it? What community nurtured and venerated it? How does its theology compare with that of Paul and the other gospel writers, Matthew, Mark, and Luke.[1]

While these issues will continue to arouse academic debate, the indisputable value of John's gospel and epistles to the devout Christian reader must not be obscured. Already in the second century Clement of Alexandria labelled John "the spiritual gospel." Within its pages lie penetrating insights into the life and teaching of Jesus Christ. The lofty heights gained by the prologue (1:1–18) alone provide reason enough to symbolize this book—as did the early church—with an eagle. In fact, medieval Christians so venerated these verses that they were read over baptized children and the seriously ill. Copies were placed in amulets worn around the neck to ward off evil!

John's gospel has endowed the theological formulations of high church councils and the devotional lives of thoughtful disciples.

---

1. While this volume is devoted exclusively to a study of the Fourth Gospel, nevertheless, frequent reference will be made to the epistles of John, which share so much in common with the Gospel.

Where else can one find the magisterial clarity with which John describes God's love for the world, the world's incongruous unbelief, and Christ's nurture of his flock as a witness of faith? The rich soil of Johannine literature stimulates the growth of clear declarations about Christ's pre-existence, divinity, and humanity. John stands shoulder to shoulder with Paul in importance and influence.

This volume is written with the beginning student in mind. New Testament scholars will at once recognize its breathtaking generalizations and omissions. Nevertheless, students who are opening the pages of the gospel for the first time deserve a guide through the maze of academic discussion. Commentaries often presuppose and contribute to these debates, leaving the novice reader in despair. Some surveys are likewise so technical that they assist only the scholar or advanced student.

Unfortunately, those of us who are professors sometimes fail to appreciate just how little of this scholarly background our students possess or will ever grasp. An outstanding student came to me the other day and said, "Why doesn't someone just show us how to do a basic literary study of a gospel? Or how to use a Greek concordance? Or how to get the most from Kittel's Theological Dictionary?"[2] He confided that, after graduation from a major evangelical seminary, most of his sermon preparation comes from William Barclay's layman's commentaries.

This book is my answer to that student. It should serve as a coach and confidant for the student just breaking in. Practical and written in an informal style, it guides to resources that primarily use the English text of the Bible for students who lack confidence in their Greek language abilities. It will also show the advanced student who has mastered Greek what research tools and techniques are best. If students find that this little book opens new insights into the exciting world of the Fourth Gospel, I will be satisfied.

I have taught courses on the Johannine literature for a number of years and each time find myself compelled to give an "introduction and overview" to the scholarly landscape. This volume presents such a prologue, followed by a rigorous exegetical study of the texts themselves. Each chapter includes bibliographical refer-

2. Gerhard Kittel, *The Theological Dictionary of the New Testament*, 9 vols., trans. by Geoffrey Bromiley (Grand Rapids: Eerdmans, 1964–1972).

ences—to studies in John or to more general reference works—so that serious students will be able to take their interests further.

Above all, I hope that this effort will uncomplicate matters for students as a map through the terrain. Maps are not always easy to read, but without them the peril of travel can be serious. Once the map is mastered, the joy of travel can be rich.

It only remains to thank the many people who have read portions of the manuscript and provided numerous constructive comments. Among these are New Testament scholars with a special interest in the subject: Robert Kysar, Raymond E. Brown, Fernando F. Segovia, Donald A. Carson, Scot McKnight, Jack Levison, David Scholer, and Klyne Snodgrass. In addition, Sonia Bodi and Norma Sutton, two professional colleagues who are research librarians in the liberal arts, evaluated the text's usefulness in the instructional setting. Paul Ingram of Baker Book House carefully and thoughtfully edited the manuscript, improving its style and substance.

Finally, I render special thanks to both seminarians and undergraduates who critiqued chapters from a student's point of view: Amy DeVries, Scott Erickson, Amy Wohl, Steve Peterson, Dan Wilson, Doug Diller, Cheryl Wendroth, and Robert Sirovatka. If students like these do not find the book stimulating and useful, then our efforts are to no avail.

Part 1

Backgrounds to the Fourth Gospel

1

History of Interpretation

My first exposure to Johannine criticism came in the autumn of 1972 at the American University of Beirut in Lebanon. As an undergraduate exchange student I was taking a course on the gospels with a French Jesuit scholar. At one point he remarked that the New Testament nowhere gives evidence that Jesus went to Samaria. I eagerly offered the Samaritan Woman story in John 4, whereupon he said, "Ah yes, but that account appears in the Fourth Gospel, and as everyone knows, John is not historically trustworthy!" Confronted by what seemed an irrefutable scholarly argument, I retreated.

When scholars reconstruct the life of Jesus, they constantly measure the quality of their sources. Is the Fourth Gospel a reliable source for the life of Jesus? We could answer with a statement of faith ("It is in the Scriptures, isn't it?"), but this confession means little in the larger marketplace of ideas. On the other hand, knowing what has been said about this Gospel—the history of its interpretation—equips us to address these academic challenges head-on. If I had done so in 1972 I would have learned that my professor was completely out of step with current Johannine scholarship.

A considerable body of New Testament literature traditionally is attributed to John: a gospel, three letters, and the Book of Revelation. A host of noncanonical writings also lay claim to his name. The legend-filled *Acts of John* provides a fictional biography of the apostle, written in the early third century. The Syriac *History of John* portrays the apostle as a magic-working evangelist. Such gnostic sources[1] as the *Gospel of Philip* quote fragments of Johannine-style sayings, while others provide accounts of his contact with Jesus, missions, and martyrdom.[2] This apocryphal literature may be set aside with ease; the biblical Johannine material has aroused more debate.

The Early Period

In the early church, the Fourth Gospel held the highest place of honor. Since it was thought to originate with the "beloved disciple" who was one of the closest to Jesus, it was esteemed to be the *most valuable* gospel. Further, John's Gospel offered a depth of insight unparalleled in the Synoptics.

Unfortunately, even the heretics loved it. A second-century gnostic writing from Egypt, the *Gospel of Truth*, shows extensive Johannine parallels. The first commentary on John's Gospel of which we are aware was written by Heracleon (c. 170–80), the most famous disciple of Valentinus, who founded the Valentinian gnostic sect. In fact, the earliest commentaries on John were all gnostic. The charismatic leader Montanus claimed to be the coming Paraclete or Comforter described in John 14–16! Because of this gnostic and Montanist interest, many orthodox leaders were reluctant to promote the Gospel. Some openly opposed its use. But where it was accepted, John was deeply revered.[3]

Irenaeus (c. 175) and some other fathers saw that John's incarnational theology could be turned on the sort of heresies being spawned in gnostic circles. When Arians depicted Jesus as a created being who was fully subordinate to the Father—and therefore much like humans—Athanasius and the Council of Nicea (325) looked to the Fourth Gospel's doctrine of Christ as an uncompromising affirmation of Jesus' divinity.[4]

---

1. *Gnostic* and *Gnosticism* (from the Gk. γνῶσις, "knowledge") refer to a complex religious movement which, in its Christian form, came into clear prominence by the second century. Sects quickly formed around prominent leaders whose teaching directly opposed that of the orthodox church.

2. Wilhelm Schneemelcher, ed., *The New Testament Apocrypha*, 2 vols., trans. A. J. Higgins, et al., eds. R. M. Wilson (Philadelphia: Westminster, 1963–1966).

3. See Martin Hengel, *The Johannine Question* (London: SCM, 1989), 1–23.

4. Maurice Wiles, *The Spiritual Gospel: The Interpretation of the Fourth Gospel in the Early Church* (Cambridge, England: Cambridge University Press, 1960); Rudolf Schnackenburg, *The*

This high respect continued through Medieval Christendom. From Augustine (354–430) to Aquinas (1224–1274) and beyond, John provided the portrait of a Jesus who directly revealed the Father. Mysticism and sacramentalism likewise found in John the language and symbolic images they enjoyed. Commentaries from this period abound.

All of this came to an abrupt end during the Enlightenment of the eighteenth and nineteenth centuries. In this period all of the Gospels came under skeptical scrutiny as European universities rejected supernatural religion. In 1778 the lecture notes of the German scholar Hermann Samuel Reimarus (1694–1768) were published. These notes denied Jesus' claim to messiahship, argued that the Gospels were later fabrications, and urged the implausibility of the resurrection. Scholars launched a brave quest to find the real Jesus of history, a rationalistic history dictated by Enlightenment standards.

Three questions were continually at issue for over 150 years after Reimarus:

1. Is the supernatural admissible as genuine history?
2. What are the relative merits of the gospels?
3. What is the essence of Jesus' message?

This third question was laden with nuances. Did Jesus preach about an ultimate crisis or catastrophe for Judaism and the world, with himself at the center (eschatology)? Indeed, did Jesus even claim to be the Son of God or the Messiah?

John's Gospel again enjoyed some favor among those who rejected orthodoxy because it contained fewer miracles and reported that Jesus gave lengthy Socratic discourses. Karl Hase (1800–1890) argued that the Johannine miracle stories seemed more authentic and less prone to embellishment. Friedrich Schleiermacher (1768–1834) embraced John fully in lectures given in 1832 and published in 1864. John is an eyewitness, Schleiermacher main-

---

Gospel According to St. John, 3 vols. (New York: Seabury, 1979), 1:193–210; J. N. D. Kelly, *Early Christian Doctrines* (New York: Harper and Row, 1978), 52–79, 223–51. See the thorough, though now-dated, bibliography by E. Malatesta, "John in the History of Exegesis," in *St. John's Gospel, 1920–1965* (Rome: Pontifical Institute, 1967): 157–71. For an appreciation of John's incarnational theology, see E. Harrison, "A Study of John 1:14," in Robert Guelich, ed., *Unity and Diversity in New Testament Theology* (Grand Rapids: Eerdmans, 1978), 23–36; and Marianne Meye-Thompson, *The Humanity of Jesus in the Fourth Gospel* (Philadelphia: Fortress, 1988).

tained, who gives us a Jesus of depth and substance. John offered
something that resonated in the nineteenth-century liberal soul.

But critical objections were soon to follow. In 1835 David F.
Strauss (1808–1874) forced the Johannine question in his influential
The Life of Christ. Strauss believed that each Gospel writer pro-
moted a preconceived theological portrait of Jesus, rendering the
Gospel presentations unhistorical. He believed this to be especially
true of John. This Gospel was inferior because it served a literary
schema and was influenced by second-century dogmas. Strauss
pointed to John's baptismal narrative (1:29–34), the calling of the
first disciples (1:35–51), and especially the absence of any mention
of Jesus' "Gethsemane struggle" to show that the Fourth Gospel
was the conscious result of "devotional, but unhistorical embellishment."[5] He even showed how the language of Jesus in the
Fourth Gospel was *John's own language* by comparing it with the
Johannine Epistles! Strauss compelled New Testament scholars to
choose between John and the Synoptics on the grounds that their
differences were utterly irreconcilable.

At Germany's Tübingen University Strauss had studied with
Ferdinand Christian Baur (1792–1860).[6] It was Baur who propelled
Strauss into biblical criticism, and it was Baur who sealed the fate
of John among scholars for years to come. Baur and what came to
be known as the "Tübingen School" drew deeply from the well of
Hegelian philosophy.

Georg Hegel (1770–1831) asserted that the dialectic of thesis,
antithesis, and synthesis fueled all of history. For example, major
movements (thesis) are often met with opposition (antithesis) and
their conflict eventually results in a synthesis. Baur applied this
sweeping framework to early Christianity. Judaism and Hellenism
had intermingled to produce Christianity. Baur went to exagger-
ated lengths to emphasize how Jewish elements in the church
(Peter) opposed Greek interests (Paul), resulting in a consensus—

---

5. David F. Strauss, as cited in Werner Georg Kümmel, *The New Testament: The History of the
Investigation of Its Problems* (E.T., Nashville: Abingdon: 1972), 126; see Albert Schweitzer, *The
Quest for the Historical Jesus* (E.T., London: A. and C. Black, 1954), 85–88.
6. Stephen C. Neill, *The Interpretation of the New Testament, 1861–1986*, 2d ed. (New York:
Oxford University Press, 1988), 20–29. Baur was viewed as a colossal scholar by his German
peers. He was at his desk at 4 every morning. During his lifetime his published works amounted
to ten thousand pages. After his death another six thousand pages were published from lectures
and notes. This is the same as writing a four-hundred-page book every year for forty years!

early Catholicism. He elaborately organized the New Testament documents around this process: Romans, 1 Corinthians, 2 Corinthians, and Galatians were Paul's gentile-Christian salvos; Matthew and the Apocalypse the Jewish-Christian responses. Acts and the Pastoral Epistles were documents of reconciliation and consensus.

What about the Fourth Gospel? Baur believed that John issued from a Greek community (thus its Hellenistic accent) that had been permeated by Jewish interests. A later writing, dated possibly 150–70, represented the reconciliation of early Christianity with its diversity. It reflected neither the apostolic circle nor the Palestinian Judaism of Jesus' day.

For the balance of the nineteenth century, criticism of the Fourth Gospel along the lines of Strauss and Baur continued unabated. Refinements to the thesis surfaced, but the broad contours remained. Many objected, especially outside of Germany. At Trinity College in Cambridge University, J. B. Lightfoot (1828–1889) dismantled Baur's reconstruction of early Christian history through an exhaustive study of the patristic fathers.[7] His colleague, Brooke Foss Westcott (1825–1901), defended the Gospel's apostolic origins in an 1882 commentary.[8] In Germany, Adolf Schlatter (1852–1938) dissented from Baur in *Die Sprache und Heimat des 4. Evangelisten* [*The Language and Province of the Fourth Gospel*] (1902) and *Der Evangelist Johannes, wie er spricht, denkt, und glaubt* [*The Fourth Evangelist: His Speech, Thought, and Belief*] (1930). Nevertheless, for many the Fourth Gospel never survived the nineteenth century as a trustworthy source.

Two important conclusions from that period still have influence. First, the Synoptics, rather than John, are viewed as the primary evidence for the life of Jesus. The reasoning confines John's interest to theology, not history. The Fourth Gospel presents an "idea" of Jesus (a myth, Strauss called it) and cannot be seen as an historical account. Second, the cultural setting of John is Hellenistic rather than Jewish since it was penned by a second-century Christian community far removed from the Jesus of Palestine. It is, quite simply, an attempt to express the Gospel in the terms of Greek philosophy.

---

7. *The Apostolic Fathers*, trans. and ed., J. B. Lightfoot and J. R. Harmer (London: MacMillan, 1889; 2d ed., M. W. Holmes, ed. and trans., Grand Rapids: Baker, 1992).

8. Brooke Foss Westcott, *Commentary According to St. John: The Authorized Version with Notes* (London: John Murray, 1882; repr. ed., Grand Rapids: Eerdmans, 1973).

In 1910 William Sanday of Oxford University chronicled this severe trend in biblical studies in his volume, *The Criticism of the Fourth Gospel*.[9] Sanday uncovered serious prejudice against John and summed up the period as "an uncompromising rejection" of the Fourth Gospel. He reported that the trend among scholars was to conceive of John as an intermediate step between Paul and gnosticism, a purer expression of Paul's Gospel, freed from any link to Judaism and the historical events in the life and death of Jesus.

The Jewishness of John

Sometimes a persistent academic thesis is broadsided from an utterly unexpected direction. In 1924 Israel Abrahams, a rabbinics scholar at Cambridge and an orthodox Jew, addressed stunning news to the university's theological society: "To us Jews, the Fourth Gospel is the most Jewish of the four!"[10]

Even a cursory reading of John reveals what Abrahams saw clearly. Does not the Gospel contain numerous allusions to the Old Testament? Do not semitic hints abound? If this is so, what happens to Baur and the Tübingen thesis? Is it right to view John as the product of the second-century Greek Christian Church?

Lightfoot and Schlatter had suggested that John's most cogent interpretation develops through rabbinic literature and the Old Testament.[11] John uses numerous references to the Old Testament, many of which are dissimilar to, say, Matthew's citations. Further, these Old Testament allusions seem to assume that readers know the references (compare chap. 10 with Ezek. 34 and 3:14 with Num. 21:9).[12] Similarly, the discourses of Jesus presuppose knowledge of the theological symbolism behind the Jewish festivals (Passover, 6:25–59; Tabernacles, chap. 7; Dedication or Hanukkah, 10:22–39).

---

9. The Morse Foundation Lectures for 1904, Union Theological Seminary (New York: Scribner's Sons, 1905).

10. Neill, *Interpretation*, 338.

11. In 1925 Marie-Joseph Lagrange, founder of the Ecole Biblique in Jerusalem, published a widely influential commentary along these lines. See Jerome Murphy-O'Connor, *The Ecole Biblique and the New Testament* (Cedar Falls, Iowa: Freiburg, 1990), 22–25.

12. See C. K. Barrett, "The Old Testament in the Fourth Gospel," *Journal of Theological Studies* 48 (1947): 155–69; D. A. Carson, "John and the Johannine Epistles," in D. A. Carson and H. G. M. Williamson, eds., *It is Written: Scripture Citing Scripture: Essays in Honor of Barnabas Lindars* (London: Cambridge University Press, 1988): 245–64.

Jesus employs rabbinic arguments in debating opponents in 5:31–47. John 6:26–59 is a midrash (or Jewish commentary) on the "bread from heaven" promised in Exodus 16:4, while 10:34–38 is a midrash on Psalm 82:6. This is hardly the sort of literature one would expect from a Greek community. On the other hand, it has been argued that John uses language dissimilar to that of Judaism. His dualism (light and darkness; above and below) and abstract expressions (truth, faith, spirit) are unlike anything in Jewish literature. But in the 1940s archaeologists uncovered the Dead Sea Scrolls at Qumran and learned from them of a Jewish sectarian community contemporary to Jesus which expressed itself in language quite similar to that found in John.

In 1922 Charles Fox Burney of Oxford advanced the thesis that, not only was John influenced by Semitic concepts, but the text had originally been written in Aramaic![13] Its language, argued Burney, betrays an Aramaic original that had been translated into Greek. This explains the simple, often wooden, Greek usage. Similarly, in 1967 Matthew Black of St. Andrews, Scotland, suggested that the Fourth Gospel's language is evidence of an author writing in Greek whose native tongue is Aramaic.[14]

John also seems to understand intimately the customs, culture, and land of first-century Palestine. Note how in 4:4–26 he casually describes Samaria and its outlook. In 5:1–2 he mentions the five-portico pool of Bethesda. Near the Church of Saint Anne in Jerusalem remains of what probably were those porticos now have been found beside pools uncovered at the turn of the century.[15] The geography of Palestine is accurately set out, as are Jewish festivals. John even describes incidental details of the temple (for example in 8:20), although the structure was destroyed by the Romans in A.D. 70.

Finally, Greek papyrus fragments[16] have come to light, providing very early portions of the New Testament. In fact, we possess seventeen papyrus fragments of John, more than have been found

---

13. Charles Fox Burney, *The Aramaic Origin of the Fourth Gospel* (Oxford, England: Clarendon, 1922).

14. Matthew Black, *An Aramaic Approach to the Gospels and Acts* (Oxford, England: Clarendon, 1967).

15. Earlier writers, commenting on these details in John 5, interpreted them symbolically, suggesting that the five porticos (porches) were the five books of Moses.

16. Papyrus is a reed that grows in the Egyptian wetlands of the Nile Delta. It was flattened, pressed, woven and smoothed to make a writing "parchment."

for any other New Testament book. An Egyptian fragment (p[52])
of about five verses from John 18 was discovered in 1920 and published in 1935. This piece of papyrus, measuring 3.5 inches by 2.3
inches, is the oldest New Testament fragment so far uncovered
and is usually dated to 125.[17] Allowing time for its circulation
throughout the church as far as Egypt pushes the date of John into
the first century and provides a latest possible date for the auto-
graph of perhaps A.D. 80 to 95.

Even after Abraham's work no consensus was reached. Others
were pursuing different avenues of investigation, still convinced
that John was a by-product of pagan mysticism and Hellenistic
gnosticism. In 1903 Alfred Loisy (1857–1940) published a commentary along these lines.[18] At Tübingen research sought to discover a "history of religions" that defined how one faith evolved
into newer forms. Such scholars as Richard Reitzenstein
(1861–1931) popularized a theory that Christianity grew from Hellenistic mystery religions and the writings of the Mandeans, then
recently discovered.[19] A myth of a "descending redeemer" had
been popular in the Near East; John integrated Jesus into its drama.
It was only left for Rudolf Bultmann (1884–1972), the great Mar-
burg professor, to make compelling use of these sources in his
magisterial commentary on John in 1941 (E.T., 1971). Bultmann's
influence on Johannine studies is still significant.[20] In 1980 (E.T.,
1984) Ernst Haenchen relied on Bultmann's outlook in his two-
volume commentary on John.[21]

Among many scholars the question of John's Jewish roots
remains unanswered. But it is an essential question as we seek the
Gospel's date and origin. A Jewish background moves the Fourth

17. For a detailed study, see Jack Finegan, *Encountering New Testament Manuscripts: A Working Introduction to Textual Criticism* (Grand Rapids: Eerdmans, 1974), 85–90; see also Victor
Salmon, *The Fourth Gospel: A History of the Textual Tradition of the Original Greek Gospel*, trans. M.
J. O'Connell (Collegeville, Minn.: Liturgical, 1976).
18. Alfred F. Loisy, *Le quatrième Évangile* (rev. ed., Paris: Emile Nourry, 1903; 2d ed., Nourry,
1921).
19. Richard Reitenstein, *Hellenistic Mystery Religions* (1956; trans. John E. Steely, Pittsburg:
Pickwick, 1978). The Mandeans (or Mandaeans) are a people of rural Iraq and Iran who claim
that John the Baptist was the messiah and are highly critical of orthodox Christianity. This sect
is the only form of ancient gnosticism that survives.
20. Bultmann's commentary is still in print (Philadelphia: Westminster, 1971) and widely
influential. The influence of Bultmann regarding these Hellenistic sources in the interpretation of John can be seen recently in Helmut Koester, *Introduction to the New Testament*, 2 vols.
(Philadelphia: Fortress, 1982): vol. 2, *History and Literature of Early Christianity*, 178–98.
21. *A Commentary on the Gospel of John*, trans. R. W. Funk (Philadelphia: Fortress, 1984).

Gospel away from Hellenistic religion and back into the world of first-century Judaism. This may have been a Judaism significantly influenced by Hellenistic thinking. It was, nevertheless, a by-product of the world of Jesus and his apostles.

Historical Traditions in John

John's cultural setting has been a vexing issue throughout the twentieth century, but possibly more important are other questions: Did John's account of the life of Jesus contain any historical data? If so, what was the relation of this data to the Synoptic Gospels?

Scholars had determined that the accounts of Matthew, Mark, and Luke were dependent on one another. This resulted in a complex literary puzzle that even today enjoys considerable attention. At the turn of the century most assumed that, since John was the last Gospel written, its author knew and used the Synoptics.[22] Implicit in this hypothesis was the rule that when a story in John paralleled, say, Mark, the account was deemed trustworthy. When it diverged from the Synoptics its historical value plummeted.

We need to look closely at this subject to gain some perspective of its importance. Westcott estimated that 93 percent of Mark could be found hidden in Matthew and Luke. But John was different. Only 8 percent of John's content paralleled the Synoptics; 92 percent was unique to the Johannine story.[23] For instance, the cleansing of the temple can be found in John 2:14–22, Matthew 21:12–13, Mark 11:15–17, and Luke 19:45–46. The feeding of the five thousand (John 6:1–14) appears in all four. But such major accounts as the dialogue with Nicodemus (3:1–21), the Samaritan woman (4:4–26), the raising of Lazarus (11:1–44), and Jesus' upper-room discourses (chaps. 13–16) all are absent from the Synoptics. Does this mean John invented them? And when we look closely at the parallel material, discrepancies appear. John records the cleansing of the temple at the beginning of Jesus' ministry, while the Syn-

---

22. Burnett Hillman Streeter, *The Four Gospels: A Study of Origins* (New York: Macmillan, 1925); more recently, see Craig Blomberg, *The Historical Reliability of the Gospels* (Downers Grove, Ill.: Inter-Varsity, 1987), 153–89.

23. Most synopses compare only the Synoptics. However, attempts to study the Johannine material are available. See especially H. F. D. Sparks, *The Johannine Synopsis of the Gospels* (New York: Harper and Row, 1974), and Kurt Aland, *Synopsis of the Four Gospels* (E.T., Stuttgart, Germany: United Bible Society, 1971; Gk. T., United Bible Society, 1975). See chapter 5.

optics put it at the end. Even the feeding miracle is ended in John with a lengthy monologue about Jesus as the "bread of life" (6:25–59). When John used the Synoptics did he he freely embellish their narratives? If this was his tendency then stories found only in John, such as Jesus' private discussion with Pilate (18:28–19:16) also must fall by the wayside.

The thesis deserves restating: if John knew and used the Synoptics, then his divergences make him suspect. Such was the view of John until 1938 when Percival Gardner-Smith wrote a critique of the evidence that John even knew about the Synoptics.[24] Gardner-Smith demonstrated the fragility of the arguments for dependency, and his criticisms have not been convincingly refuted. Scholars began to ask whether John's accounts stemmed from independent traditions that *antedated* the Synoptics. In 1953 C. H. Dodd concluded *The Interpretation of the Fourth Gospel* with an appendix rejecting the "symbolic" use of place names in John. He concluded that the Gospel may contain original traditional narratives associated with southern Palestine. Place names such as Bethesda are indeed geographical locations. He wrote: "The *prima facie* impression is that John is, in large measure at any rate, working independently of other written gospels."[25]

In 1963 Dodd offered a full-fledged study, boldly entitling it *Historical Tradition in the Fourth Gospel*. This volume was a watershed in Johannine studies in which Dodd concluded that "behind the Fourth Gospel lies an ancient tradition independent of the other gospels, and meriting serious consideration as a contribution to our knowledge of the historical facts concerning Jesus Christ."[26] Dodd began with a thorough study of the passion narrative and concluded that, rather than a reshuffling of the Synoptics, John's story was ancient, Jewish, possibly dated before A.D. 70, and even "better informed than the tradition behind the Synoptics!"[27]

---

24. *St. John and the Synoptic Gospels* (Cambridge, England: Cambridge University Press).
25. Neill, *Interpretation*, 449
26. C. H. Dodd, *Historical Tradition in the Fourth Gospel* (New York: Cambridge University Press, 1963), 423. For a critique of Dodd, see D. A. Carson, "Historical Tradition in the Fourth Gospel: After Dodd, What?" in R. T. France and David Wenham, *Gospel Perspectives: Studies of History and Tradition in the Four Gospels* (Sheffield, England: JSOR, 1981), 83–145.
27. Dodd, *Historical Tradition*, 120; so too, Thomas Walter Manson, "Materials for the Life of Jesus in the Fourth Gospel," in T. W. Manson, *Studies in the Gospels and Epistles*, ed. M. Black (Philadelphia: Westminister, 1962): 105–22

It goes without saying that scholarly unanimity has not been reached on this subject either. In 1978 C. K. Barrett published the second edition of his 1955 commentary, still defending—even defensively—his view that John was familiar with Mark (and possibly even Luke) and had minimal historical value.[28] Robert H. Lightfoot's (1883–1953) commentary published in 1956[29] claimed that John knew all three Synoptic Gospels. But these views are not winning the day. Writers are now inclined to say that John records ancient traditions from the same wellspring as that of the Synoptics. Occasionally he shares these primitive traditions with the Synoptics, but he does not employ the Synoptics themselves.[30]

The importance of this shift cannot be missed. As Gardner-Smith wrote in 1938, "If in the Fourth Gospel we have a survival of the type of first century Christianity which owed nothing to synoptic developments, and which originated in quite a different intellectual atmosphere, its historical value may be very great indeed."[31] Indeed impressive new light has been shed on the Fourth Gospel making it an *independent, authoritative* witness to the traditions about Jesus on a par with any historical claims found in the Synoptics.

The New Look on the Fourth Gospel

Many writers have chronicled these developments, but none was so famous as J. A. T. Robinson (1919–1983) of Trinity College, Cambridge. In 1957 Robinson announced a *new look* on the Fourth Gospel in a paper read at Oxford.[32] In it he described an *old look* on John that was under siege. The old look consisted of five major propositions:

1. John is dependent on sources, in particular the Synoptics.
2. John's background is different from that of its subjects.

---

28. *The Gospel According to St. John: An Introduction with Commentary and Notes on the Gospel Text* (Philadelphia: Westminster, 1978). See also C. K. Barrett, "John and the Synoptic Gospels," *Expository Times* 85 (1973–1974): 228–33

29. *St. John's Gospel* (Oxford, England: Clarendon, 1956).

30. See the recent remarks of Stephen S. Smalley, "Keeping Up With Recent Studies: St. John's Gospel," *Expository Times* 96 (1986–1987): 103; compare with D. Moody Smith, *Johannine Christianity* (New York: Columbia University Press, 1984).

31. Percival Gardner-Smith, *Saint John and the Synoptic Gospels* (Cambridge, England: Cambridge University Press, 1938), 96, as cited in Lightfoot, *St. John's Gospel*, 29.

32. Published in *Studia Evangelica, TU*, 73 (1959): 338–50; see also in J. A. T. Robinson, *Twelve New Testament Studies* (Naperville, Ill.: A. R. Allenson, 1962).

The author was a Greek, writing with significant gnostic
influence.
3. John is not a serious witness to the Jesus of history.
4. John shows evidence of a late first-century theological
   development.
5. The author of the Fourth Gospel is not the apostle John
   nor an eyewitness.

Robinson went on to outline the demise of these views, illus-
trating how they all interlock. The new look not only overturns
these propositions; it affirms a genuine connection between the
fourth evangelist and historical traditions about Jesus. Those
embracing the new look must debate questions about date, cultural
background, and authorship within the locale of early first-century
Jewish Christianity. In sum, the new look earnestly affirms the value
of the Johannine tradition. The presumption no longer holds that
John fails to merit the historical trustworthiness of its synoptic peers.

The new look's insistence on John's independence from the Synoptics and John's Jewish orientation has been well received. But
the proposal that John offers genuine history has resulted from a
more realistic appraisal of all four Gospels. Each evangelist presents theology along with history and "interprets" Jesus for readers. For example, Luke shapes the portrait of Jesus in unique ways,
as does John. But this in no way disparages the historical value of
Luke or any other canonical Gospel.

In the 1970s Robinson's interest in John led him to reread
Dodd's *Historical Tradition in the Fourth Gospel*. He was forced to
rethink not only the date of John but of the entire New Testament,
publishing *Redating the New Testament* in 1976. He even suggested
that John could have been penned during the 60s. Why? John is
conspicuously silent about the doom of Jerusalem, which the
Romans razed in 70, and he presupposes a pre-70 outlook (see
2:19–20; 11:47–52). John employs details of the city as if it were still
standing (see 5:2). Added to this is the widespread evidence,
defended also by Dodd, that John is aware of the "psychological
divisions of Palestine before the war." This "would be barely intel-
ligible outside a purely Jewish context in the earliest period."[33]
Robinson poured the last years of his life into Johannine scholar-

---

33. J. A. T. Robinson, *Redating the New Testament*, (Philadelphia: Westminster, 1976), 264.

ship. His final volume, *The Priority of John* (1985), is a massive compilation of his conservative, unconventional views. This exhaustive defense of John's antiquity, authority, and Jewish orientation argues what its title suggests. It epitomized the new look that Robinson had signalled thirty years earlier.[34]

We quickly add that not all scholars have agreed with these results. *The Priority of John* has been given scant attention in those academic circles that remain convinced that John is a significantly late Gospel whose heritage is Hellenistic.[35]

The Significance of the New Look

The issues we have been discussing are important because they directly affect the way we value and interpret the Gospel of John. We are forced to make decisions. If we conclude that the cultural background is Hellenistic, as do Bultmann, Haenchen, and to a degree Barrett, the miracle at Cana where Jesus turns water into wine may reflect a Christianizing of the Greek Dionysus myth. On the other hand, if it arises from early Palestinian Judaism we shall need to look to Old Testament and Jewish antecedents, as do John Marsh, Raymond E. Brown, Leon Morris, and George R. Beasley-Murray.

The same is true for the value of the Johannine traditions. It is not enough to accept merely those accounts which parallel the Synoptics. As Stephen S. Smalley urges, "we can now reckon seriously with the possibility that the Fourth Gospel, including John's special material, is grounded in historical tradition when it *departs* from the synoptics *as well as* when it overlaps them."[36] Hence, exclusively Johannine stories, such as Nicodemus, the Samaritan woman, and Lazarus, must no longer be viewed as fictional. They bear important historical worth.

Sometimes it is helpful to illustrate the conscious choice before us. The new look urges that we view the Gospel as Jewish and historically reliable. This view has not always carried the day and is

---

34. J. A. T. Robinson, *The Priority of John* (North American ed., Yorktown Heights, N.Y.: Meyer-Stone, 1987). Typical of this trend is C. F. Coakley, "The Anointing at Bethany and the Priority of John," *Journal of Biblical Literature* 102 (1988): 241–56.

35. See, for example, Gerald S. Sloyan, *What Are They Saying about John?* (New York: Paulist, 1991).

36. Stephen S. Smalley, *John: Evangelist and Interpreter* (Greenwood, S.C.: Attic, 1978), 29.

fig. 1

A New Way of Looking at the Gospel of John

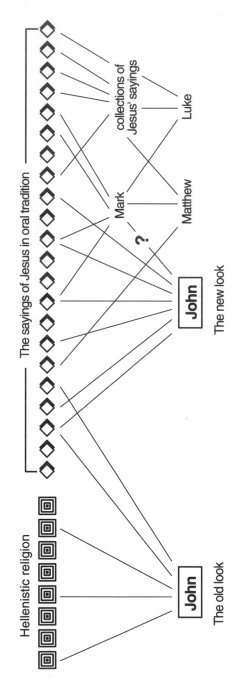

The old look affirmed a strong link between the Fourth Gospel and Hellenistic religion with minimal dependence on the pre-Synoptic traditions. The new look urges that John employs these traditions, is Jewish, and may even have originated its earliest stories from the apostolic period. Thus John has a high claim to historicity, even when the Gospel does not parallel Matthew, Mark, or Luke. Some scholars even wonder if John knew and used the Synoptics in some form. For instance, did John know early editions of Mark or maybe Luke?

seriously disputed, but it has many serious adherents, whose views are not to be dismissed lightly and whose numbers are growing steadily.

In the illustration, note the significant connections. The old look on John finds its sources either within the synoptic tradition or within Hellenism. The new look points either to sources *shared* with the synoptic tradition or with authentic independent traditions. For example, one box might represent the story of the feeding of the five thousand used by both Mark and John. Another box might represent the story of Nicodemus, a narrative unused by Mark but included in John. To be sure, this simplifies matters considerably. One may find, without difficulty, scholars who defend these influences on John.

Current Trends

The question of John's historicity (and thereby the Gospel's authenticity) is certainly an important issue. But for some, especially those outside the evangelical camp, these questions are no longer pressing. New trends in Johannine research are following other movements in biblical studies and in literary criticism. The following are some of these trends?

Source Criticism

A compelling interest among many Johannine scholars today is the quest to unravel the literary structure of the Fourth Gospel. The Gospel has left us some evidence showing traces of its own history. For instance, 2:11 and 4:54 record a numbered sequence for the signs of Jesus, but these numbers do not always seem consistent. Throughout the first half of the Gospel, discourses seem related to these signs according to a pattern. Evidence further suggests that John is irregularly stitched together, sometimes interrupting the flow of narrative. Consider Jesus' movements as he bounces between Galilee and Judea in chapters 3–7.

Robert T. Fortna has taken the lead in seeking the *literary seams* in the Gospel—thus distinguishing John's sources.[37] We shall devote

---

37. Robert T. Fortna, *The Gospel of Signs: A Reconstruction of the Narrative Source Underlying the Fourth Gospel* (London: Cambridge University Press, 1970); idem, *The Fourth Gospel and Its Predecessor: From Narrative Source to Present Gospel* (Philadelphia: Fortress, 1988).

chapter 3 to the suggestions of this important area of research. Since Fortna has undoubtedly set the agenda for future investigation, we must be careful to ask critical questions about his presuppositions. There is room for critical evaluation. For example, source criticism seeks to gather evidences of trustworthy historical data that lie behind the text. The conclusion so far has been that the source for narratives of Jesus' signs is the more ancient. Yet such a view must deal with a serious problem: If sign narratives and discourses arise from separate sources, they are intricately interwoven . . . and their language is quite uniform.

Brown has done similar work. He believes that we can detect five *layers* of tradition in the Gospel, each from a separate point in the history of the book's composition.[38] While not many have rushed to endorse these reconstructions, a near-consensus seems at hand that a community of Christians did collaborate in the development and preservation of the Johannine traditions. Debate continues, however, about the degree to which this community preserved, shaped, and reinvented traditional materials.

Once again, questions must be raised with regard to the presuppositions of such a hypothesis. It is the tacit understanding of Brown, Fortna, and others that the narrative of the Fourth Gospel is telling us more about the history of the Johannine community (its "lives, loves, and hates," as Brown puts it) than about Jesus.

Sociology and Theology

This interest in the Gospels as windows into the life and times of a particular New Testament community has been taken up by scholars with a keen interest in sociology. This trend has been with us for some time and reflects the interests of the late twentieth century to study the diversity and complexity of social organization. For instance, Bruce J. Malina examines life and values in the New Testament world by employing the categories of cultural anthropology.[39] One problem with studying the New Testament communities in this manner is that little direct evidence tells us about the

---

38. Raymond E. Brown, *The Community of the Beloved Disciple* (New York: Paulist, 1979). See a discussion of Brown's theory in chap. 3.

39. Bruce J. Malina, *The New Testament World. Insights from Cultural Anthropology* (Atlanta: John Knox, 1981); see also, Howard C. Kee, *Knowing the Truth: A Sociological Approach to New Testament Interpretation* (Minneapolis: Fortress, 1989).

character of early Christian life. The only access possible is to view the Gospels as windows, not on the life of Jesus but rather on the communities which produced them.

Johannine sociological analysis simply attempts to reconstruct the value system, community characteristics, and worldview of the Christians who produced the Fourth Gospel. David Rensberger's *Johannine Faith and Liberating Community* attempts this in a consistent and thoroughgoing fashion.[40] Thus John 3 and 9 are *communal symbols* showing the inner-tensions of the community and the severe choices each member had to make. The trial sequence in the Gospel (along with John 5) tells us about the Johannine worldview of hostility and suspicion.

Perhaps the most troubling problem with such reconstructions is that the interpreter can find in the Gospel whatever he or she is looking for. *The sociological grid may be made to fit, even when the ancient evidence is not appropriate to the study at hand.* For example, Rensberger employs the liberation theology categories of Jose Miranda to prove that the Johannine church was an "oppressed community" seeking liberation from powerful authorities. This struggle becomes the meaning of the Johannine Christology: Jesus' conflict with the Jews is simply the church's conflict with the world. In the Nicodemus narrative Nicodemus is challenged "to be born into a people"—to undertake "deliberate downward mobility" and to take a stand with the "oppressed community."[41] "Good works" in John translate into "the eschatological transformation of the world and its social systems on the basis of love and justice."[42]

While this is a compelling and fascinating suggestion, we are right to wonder if the interpreter is bringing categories to the text that may not be there. In this case, the author neglects the major themes of inwardness, individual piety, and mysticism so central to John. How do we know when we introduce our own social framework to the text?

---

40. (Philadelphia: Westminster, 1988). See review by author in *Reformed Journal*, (March 1990): 30. Rensberger offers an introductory chapter (pp. 15–36) in which he charts the development of this approach.
41. Ibid., 114.
42. Ibid., 127.

Rhetorical Criticism

If there is a cutting edge to Johannine study, many writers would like to find it in rhetorical critical analysis.[43] Scholars in this field "do not ask questions, at least primarily, about the history of the text, the state of the Johannine community, John's historical trustworthiness, or sources. Rather they ask how to make sense of the text as it stands . . ."[44] Above all, the "sense of the text" is determined as a reader interacts with the story.

The key used by these interpreters to unlock the Gospel's message is a set of communication theories—universal structures found in virtually any composition. John is viewed as a writing to which we react, which forces us to make a response as the story of Jesus unfolds.

Without doubt the most comprehensive treatment of John from this vantage belongs to Alan Culpepper in *The Anatomy of the Fourth Gospel: A Study in Literary Design*.[45] Culpepper sets out to make the first thorough rhetorical examination of the Fourth Gospel, using the interdisciplinary tools of modern literary criticism. For instance, he studies the plot, the relation between the narrator and the assumed reader, narrative time, the characters (and their relation to the narrator), and the real author (who stands behind the narration itself). We as readers are carried through the story, which unfolds as the narrator gives us hints of what is really happening. In 2:11 the narrator explains the signs and glory of Jesus. He has inside information so that we can see what the characters are thinking and feeling. And then (21:24) we suddenly are told that, indeed, this narrator is the beloved disciple, who all along has been evidencing an intimacy with Jesus in the story.

A shift is at work here in our understanding of the relation of *truth* to *historical narrative*. Biblical study for centuries has understood truth to be a value that is central to the historical facts given in the text. That is why heated debates have always raged around the historicity and Jewishness of the narratives. But here we find that truth comes in other ways as well. The novel, for instance, conveys

---

43. D. A. Carson, *The Gospel According to John* (Grand Rapids: Eerdmans, 1991), 38.
44. Ibid., 38.
45. (Philadelphia: Fortress, 1983).

truth about the realities of life, even if it is entirely fictional. *Thus truth does not have to be necessarily tied to historicity* [46] Truth-claims can still be made through a narrative which provides poor history or no history at all. In fact, it is the drama itself, the literary world that the author creates, which ushers new truth to the reader.

Serious questions must be asked of this method.[47] How appropriate is it, for one thing, to use categories developed for critiquing modern novels to interpret first-century Gospels? Evangelicals have a far more serious complaint. Culpepper says the Gospel should not be a window into the life of Jesus but a mirror in which we see ourselves reacting, learning, and discovering what the narrative gives us. Carson rightly observes that when we look through Culpepper's window "we have sacrificed the Gospel's claims to certain historical specificity, to eyewitness credibility, to the *truth claims* of this Gospel, and set sail on the shoreless sea of existential subjectivity."[48]

Conclusion

Each of the trends discussed in this chapter offers both promise and challenge to the interpreter. But any novice who looks at current literature—commentaries, monographs, or journal articles— must be aware of these trends and be able to critically evaluate them. A publisher mailed a new commentary to me recently with the intention that I review it for a journal. At a glance it was evident that the author still holds to a completely Hellenistic interpretation of John, but, finding that unsatisfying for the modern audience, looked to themes in modern liberation theology for a message. My sincere hope is that students who find this commentary in the library will see it as a volume in conversation with decades of Johannine research. . . . and since so many of its theses

---

46. See Hans W. Frei, *The Eclipse of Biblical Narrative: A Study in Eighteenth and Nineteenth Century Hermeneutics* (New Haven, Conn.: Yale University Press, 1974), and Meir Sternberg, *The Poetics of Biblical Narrative: Ideological Literature and the Drama of Reading* (Bloomington, Ind.: Indiana University Press, 1985).

47. See D. A. Carson's review of Culpepper in *Trinity Journal* 4 (1983): 122–26

48. Carson, *The Gospel*, 65.

are still being debated, that they will use such a book with care and critical insight.

Bibliography

Anderson, Charles C. *Critical Quests of Jesus*. Grand Rapids: Eerdmans, 1969.

Briggs, Robert C. *Interpreting the New Testament Today: An Introduction to Methods and Issues in the Study of the New Testament*. Nashville: Abingdon, 1973.

Brown, Colin. *Jesus in European Protestant Thought 1778–1860*. Durham, N.C.: Labyrinth, 1985.

Brown, Raymond E. "The Relation Between the Fourth Gospel and the Synoptic Gospels." In R. E. Brown, *New Testament Essays*. Milwaukee: Bruce Chapman, 1965: 143–216.

Carson, D. A., "Recent Literature on the Fourth Gospel: Some Reflections." *Themelios* 9.1 (September 1983): 8–18.

_____. "Selected Recent Studies of the Fourth Gospel." *Themelios* 14.2 (January 1989): 57–64.

Dodd, C. H. *Historical Tradition in the Fourth Gospel*. New York: Cambridge University Press, 1963.

_____. *The Interpretation of the Fourth Gospel*. Cambridge, England: Cambridge University Press, 1953.

Freed, E. D. *Old Testament Quotations in the Gospel of John*. Leiden: Brill, 1965.

Gardner-Smith, Percival. *Saint John and The Synoptic Gospels*. London: Cambridge University Press, 1938.

Henry, Patrick. *New Directions in New Testament Study*. Philadelphia: Westminster, 1979.

Higgins, Angus J. B. *The Historicity of the Fourth Gospel*. London: Lutterworth, 1960.

Hoskyns, Edwin C., and F. N. Davey. *The Fourth Gospel*. London: Faber and Faber, 1947. See pages 58–135.

Howard, Wilbert Francis. *The Fourth Gospel in Recent Criticism and Interpretation*, rev. by C. K. Barrett. London: Epworth, 1955.

Hunter, Archibald M. *According to John: The New Look at the Fourth Gospel*. Philadelphia: Westminster, 1968.

Kümmel, Werner Georg. *Introduction to the New Testament*, trans H. C. Kee. Nashville: Abingdon, 1975. See pages 196–99.

_____. *The New Testament: The History of the Investigation of Its Problems*, trans. S. M. Gilmour and H. C. Kee. Nashville: Abingdon, 1972.

Kysar, Robert. *The Fourth Evangelist and His Gospel. An Examination of Contemporary Scholarship.* Minneapolis: Augsburg, 1975.

Lindars, Barnabas. "Some Recent Trends in the Study of John." *Way* 30 (1990): 329–38

Malatesta, E. *St. John's Gospel, 1920–1965.* Rome: Pontifical Biblical Institute, 1967.

Neill, Stephen C. *The Interpretation of the New Testament 1861-1986,* 2d ed. New York: Oxford University Press, 1988.

Robinson, J. A. T. *Redating the New Testament.* Philadelphia: Westminster, 1976.

_____. *The Priority of John.* Yorktown Heights, N.Y.: Meyer-Stone, 1987.

Sanday, William. *The Criticism of the Fourth Gospel.* New York: Scribner's Sons, 1905.

Schnackenburg, Rudolf. *The Gospel According to St. John,* 3 vols., trans. K. Smith. New York: Seabury, 1979. See 1:192–217.

Schweitzer, Albert. *The Quest for the Historical Jesus.* E.T., London: A. and C. Black, 1954.

Scott, Ernest F. *The Fourth Gospel, Its Purpose and Its Theology.* Edinburgh: T. and T. Clark, 1906.

Sloyan, Gerald S. *What are They Saying about John?* New York: Paulist, 1991.

Smalley, Stephen S. *John: Evangelist and Interpreter.* Greenwood, S.C.: Attic, 1978.

Smith, D. Moody. *Johannine Christianity: Essays on Its Setting, Sources, and Theology.* Columbia, S.C.: University of South Carolina Press, 1984.

Sparks, H. F. D. *The Johannine Synopsis of the Gospels.* New York: Harper and Row, 1974.

Wiles, Maurice F. *The Spiritual Gospel: The Interpretation of the Fourth Gospel in the Early Church.* London: Cambridge University Press, 1960.

2

The Authorship
of the Fourth Gospel

A number of years ago I visited Amman, Jordan, with a friend. On the spur of the moment we decided to hitchhike with backpacks south through the desert in search of Petra, the capital of the Nabatean kingdom (well known in New Testament times). We passed through Ma'an and our driver deposited us on a deserted road that would lead us to Wadi Musa near Petra. Soon we were approached by an Arab Bedouin who lived nearby with his family and flocks. Mustafa (as we learned his name to be) led us to his home and offered us refreshments. We suspected this was leading to something when our host produced a postcard from his coat pocket. It was from Chicago and its five-year-old date explained the card's wear. "Dear Mustafa," it went, "We had a great visit to Jordan. Thanks for your hospitality. Please visit us if you come to Chicago. Sincerely, Marge and Carl Hasenjager." My Arabic was as poor as Mustafa's English, but we eventually got the message that we were to write a short letter back to Marge and Carl.

Mustafa recited everything he wanted to say and I dutifully filled in the blanks when his sentences lapsed into Arabic. But I was faithful to his intention. He wanted to express thanks, friendship, and welcome in the generous fashion so typical of Arab culture. He needed my skill to compose, pen, and address the note.

Under these circumstances it might be interesting to ask the question, "Who was the author of the letter?" In one sense it was Mustafa. He had originated it, giving it life and purpose. On the

37

other hand, I had shaped it, supplementing to respect Mustafa's desires. In a very real sense, I was serving as an ancient biblical scribe or amanuensis might have served. The literary piece was a *joint production*, with a principal author and a secondary assistant.

When scholars talk about the authorship of a biblical book they are often dealing with such complexities. It may be that *direct authorship* applies when someone such as Paul pens every word of a letter. But in the case of Paul's epistle to the Romans, the apostle employed a scribe named Tertius (16:22). What role did Tertius play? Did Paul dictate to him? Was he an intimate colleague in whom Paul placed great trust? Some scholars urge that significant scribal involvement may even pertain to Paul, as in Ephesians. We might call this arrangement *indirect authorship* when a second hand not only writes the piece, but edits and shapes it.

This question of direct versus indirect authorship goes one more step in the study of the Gospels. Scholarship has ascertained that the Gospels are collections of materials which were well formed before, say, Mark or Luke put them to use. That is, the Gospels had a *pre-history*.[1] While an individual author may have been instrumental in gathering, assembling, and arranging these materials, it is uncertain what role he played in the final product. Were his efforts later edited? Did a disciple rearrange and supplement it? In some cases scholars have argued that the Gospels were productions of communities of people and that an apostolic author never even touched the material. Apostolic authorship was a fictional supplement designed to lend authority to the writing.

The authorship of the Fourth Gospel is notoriously difficult to decipher. Four positions generally represent today's terrain:

1. *The Gospel was compiled either by John the son of Zebedee or by one of his close followers.* If John did the work, then at least a disciple edited the book since John 21:20–23 seems to make some reference to John's death.
2. *The Gospel was a devotional treatise written by a pious believer in the second century* who has written many of his own experiences back into the life of Jesus. Much like the apocryphal *Acts of John*, the writer reveals mysteries into the deeper truths about Christ.

---

1. See Scot McKnight, *Interpreting the Synoptic Gospels* (Grand Rapids: Baker, 1988).

3. *The Gospel was the production of a community of Christians* who may have possessed the Synoptics and some of Paul's letters. Their aim was to bring the reality of Jesus into their own Hellenistic experience and to create stories about Jesus which in fact describe their own experiences.
4. The fourth option is a variation of the first and third. The Apostle John may have founded a community of Christians and bequeathed to it some historical reminiscences of Jesus, but after John's death *the tradition was utterly reforged to reflect the community's own history.*

The second view is passé and the third is less in vogue, due to the current emphasis on John's independent traditions and Jewish orientation. The fourth seems most plausible to such modern critical writers as Raymond E. Brown and, to a lesser extent, George R. Beasley-Murray. Conservatives tend to defend the first position and most accept a significant amount of editorial activity, either by a disciple of John or by a community. But this opens up an important question with which conservatives must wrestle. Does the authority of the Gospel rest with the notion that John the apostle is its author? Certainty may be impossible given the evidence at hand.

At the center of this question are the very issues which informed the debate about the "new look" on John. J. A. T. Robinson saw clearly that the logical result of the new look was reopening the question about authorship. If John's date belongs in the first century, if the Gospel's cultural mileu is Jewish, and if it is a valuable witness to the Jesus of history, it is not implausible to argue for apostolic authorship. In doing so, however, we are not compelled to exclude the possibility of other editorial hands. A current Johannine scholar, Stephen S. Smalley, puts it this way: "John the Apostle, also known as the Beloved Disciple, handed on to some of his own followers his eyewitness account of the Jesus story, and in turn they were responsible for the publication of the Fourth Gospel in its finished form. Thus the work is apostolic, but not in fact *written* by the apostle."[2]

---

2. Stephen S. Smalley, "Keeping Up With Recent Studies: St. John's Gospel," *Expository Times* 96 (1986–87): 102–8.

How do we determine the authorship of a document almost two thousand years old? First, we look inside it for *internal evidence* of the author's hand. Second, we examine what other writers not far-removed from John had to say. This is *external evidence*, and in the case of the Fourth Gospel there is an abundance. Our task, then, is to sift the clues from these sources to see if we can accumulate sufficient evidence for the author's identity.

Internal Evidence

The earliest complete Greek manuscripts of John employ the heading "Κατα Ιωαννην" ("according to John"). But this is anonymous. Which John is meant? John the Baptist is the only John named in the Gospel, and he assuredly is not the author.[3] The obvious John to consider is the brother of James, son of Zebedee, who features prominently in the Synoptics (Mark 1:19–20). But nowhere is this person mentioned! In John 21:2 the "sons of Zebedee" are listed (showing that James and John were known) but the name *John* is never provided. The curious absence of any reference to this apostle increases the mystery of the puzzle.

The best evidence comes from an anonymous figure described as "the beloved disciple" (13:23; 19:26; 20:2; 21:7, 20). We can assume that John's readers know this disciple's name. Perhaps it is a title of respect or veneration. The same is true of the mother of Jesus. Nowhere is she named Mary—and if the Fourth Gospel were our only source, she would never have been known by name. Something similar is evidenced in the Dead Sea Scrolls of Qumran. That community's leader was "The Teacher of Righteousness," but nowhere in the Qumran literature is he named.

The beloved disciple first appears in the upper room before Jesus' arrest (13:21–30). The Synoptics make clear that this meal was reserved for the Twelve (Mark 14:17), and so we may be able to deduce that the beloved disciple must have been an apostle. He also reclined next to Jesus and was able to lean back easily against Jesus to ask the name of the traitor in their company. The text

---

3. The earliest full preface to the Gospel belongs to the Muratorian Canon (c 180–200). This lengthy addition gives a fantastic but fictional rendition of the Gospel's origin from John, the son of Zebedee (quoted below).

shows intimacy and suggests that the beloved disciple knew Jesus well and could make inquiries for the other eleven.

John 19:26 shows him standing at the foot of the cross with Jesus' mother. Jesus indicates to this disciple that he is now to care for Jesus' mother. If 19:25–26 is compared with the same account found in Matthew 27:56, it appears that Jesus' "mother's sister" (Mary's sister or Jesus' aunt) may be the same as the "mother of the sons of Zebedee." This would make John the maternal cousin of Jesus and explain why the apostle is assigned to care for Mary.[4] This connection, however, presupposes that the beloved disciple is a son of Zebedee. At least the logic of this explanation makes for an intriguing explanation of 19:26.

On Easter morning Peter and the beloved disciple race to the empty tomb (20:2–10). The account shows the disciple having great virtue: he outruns Peter, sees the evidence, and even though Peter enters the tomb first, the beloved disciple is first to "see and believe." Obviously the readers of this Gospel are to view the beloved disciple as a model of virtue and faith.

The comparison of the beloved disciple to Peter comes up again in chapter 21. He alone identifies the resurrected Jesus on the shore (21:4–7) and though Peter sprints to Jesus' side, the beloved disciple stays with the miraculous catch. This leads to Jesus' inquiries about Peter's love (21:15–17) and an oblique description of Peter's martyrdom (21:18–19).

Perhaps the most important reference is found in 21:20–24. The fate of the beloved disciple becomes a natural subject following the discussion in 21:18–19 about Peter's death. But it appears that a well-known saying of Jesus was subject to considerable misunderstanding ("If it is my will that he remain until I come, what is that to you?" 21:22 NRSV). Apparently the popular view was that the beloved disciple would not die, but would witness Christ's second coming personally. Now in light of the beloved disciple's apparent death, 21:23 must make the correction explicit.

This brings us to 21:24, according to many (such as Brooke Foss Westcott and Henry P. V. Nunn) the earliest evidence of author-

---

4. This alignment is very well-known but far from certain. See John Henry Bernard, *Critical and Exegetical Commentary on the Gospel According to St. John*, 2 vols., ed. A. H. McNeile (New York: Scribner's Sons, 1929), 1:xxxv; and Raymond E. Brown, *The Gospel According to John*, 2 vols., in Anchor Bible Commentaries (New York: Doubleday, 1966–1970), 1:xcvii and 2:905–6.

ship. "This is the disciple [the beloved disciple] who is bearing witness to these things—and who has written these things." Despite
his death the beloved disciple, nevertheless, continued to nurture
his followers by providing the Gospel itself as a written testimony
to the life of Jesus. Now his disciples pen a final credit to him, complete with words of respect: "and we know that his testimony is
true." These verses apply not just to the previous verses in chapter 21, but to the entire Gospel. The beloved disciple is the eyewitness source to the Fourth Gospel's testimony. Note the language
of the text carefully: The beloved disciple is the source of testimony
as an *eyewitness* and he authored (ὁ γράψας) something as a record.
Nevertheless, other participants or editors have shown their hands.

Indirect references to this disciple may lie in other texts as well.
John 19:34–37 corroborates the role of the beloved disciple in 21:24.
Here an unnamed disciple bears witness to the events of the cross.
19:35 makes his eyewitness role explicit, "He who saw it has born
witness—his testimony is true and he knows that he tells the
truth." Of course we cannot be certain whether or not this is also
the beloved disciple in 19:35, and there is no suggestion of authorship. Still, the text relates that the story we read originated from
an eyewitness tradition—someone who was there and who later
gave a report. This verification holds striking similarities to that
in 21:24 and urges that they point to the same person.

More evidence of a prominent unnamed disciple occurs in two
other places. In 18:15–16 it is "another disciple" who gains access
for Peter to the high priest's courtyard. Is the reader meant to
understand that this is the beloved disciple? It would seem unlikely
that one of the Twelve would be a personal acquaintance of the
high priest.[5] Then again, the close connection with Peter here
reminds us of the two narratives we have already seen in which
the beloved disciple and Peter play a complementary role (20:1–10;
21:4–8). From a literary standpoint we cannot exclude this as a possible reference to the beloved disciple.

---

5. We do know that Mary was related to Elizabeth, wife of Zechariah the priest (Luke 1:36,
ἡ συγγενίς, a female relative but not necessarily a cousin) giving the family a priestly connection
(Luke 1:5). If John's aunt is Mary, he too may have had a similar connection. At least the possibility of a priestly link to John is not implausible. See the confidence of C. F. Dodd in this
regard, *Historical Tradition in the Fourth Gospel* (New York: Cambridge University Press, 1963),
86–88.

A similar occasion appears in 1:35–42. Who is the unnamed disciple with Andrew? Presumably he too has a brother since one reading of verse 41 suggests that Andrew was the first to find his brother. Evidence connecting this passage to the other texts is slim however.

We now must ask, who are the best candidates to be identified as the beloved disciple? Bultmann suggested that this was no historical person at all but a literary figure—an ideal disciple offered as a model to the reader. Certainly the beloved disciple is held aloft as an exemplary Christian, but he does play another role. He is the foundational witness to the Gospel's historical tradition. One way or another, he must be a genuine person.

Nominees have been legion. Among them, Lazarus deserves special mention. If we use only the Gospel itself as a source, he is the one man of whom it is said that Jesus specifically "loved" (11:3, 11, 36). The beloved disciple passages also occur *after* the Lazarus episode (chapter 11). But why would the text mention him by name in chapter 11 and thereafter disguise it? Further, chapter 13 says the beloved disciple was at Jesus' Passover meal; since Lazarus was not one of the Twelve, it is uncertain that he was present.[6] This proposal does have intriguing literary support from within the Gospel. In chapter 21, there is some confusion about why the beloved disciple might die. If this were Lazarus, this might be written with reference to chapter 11—Lazarus had already experienced a "resurrection," so would he not be impervious to death? Jesus had said in Bethany, "I am the resurrection and the life, those who believe in me, *even though they die*, will live, and everyone who lives and believes in me *will never die*" (11:25–26 NRSV). Since the Lazarus episode is at the literary center of the Gospel and is a clear parallel to the story of Jesus' death and resurrection in chapters 19 and 20, it should not surprise us to learn that its hero is the source of the Fourth Gospel.

John Mark is another well-known candidate (Acts 12:12; Philemon 24). He lived in Jerusalem and would know southern Judah well, as the Gospel certainly does. Mark is associated with Peter (Acts 12:12; 1 Pet. 5:13), which may explain the Gospel's rivalry between Peter and the beloved disciple. He even had priestly con-

---

6. The current defense of the Lazarus theory can be found in Vernard Eller, *The Beloved Disciple: His Name, His Story, His Thought* (Grand Rapids: Eerdmans, 1987).

nections, since Barnabas *the Levite* was his cousin (Col. 4:10). But
John Mark also was not a member of the Twelve. And tradition
has associated him with the writing of the second Gospel.

This leaves John, the son of Zebedee, as the most promising candidate:

1. *He was one of the Twelve.* In the Synoptics he, Peter, and
   James formed an inner circle around Jesus. This would
   explain the intimacy of John's picture of Jesus.
2. *In the Synoptics John most often appears with Peter,* and this continues in Acts. They arrange the details of the Last Supper
   (Luke 22:8). Later they are together in Jerusalem (Acts 3:1,
   11) and are placed in custody together (Acts 4), boldly speaking to the Sanhedrin (4:13). They reappear in Samaria as
   envoys from Jerusalem (8:14). In Galatians 2:9 Paul describes
   John, with Peter and James, as pillars of the church. Thus,
   the comparison with Peter in the Fourth Gospel is not out
   of character.
3. *The Gospel normally refers to disciples by name but John is not
   listed among them.* This unusual silence is explained if the
   beloved disciple is concealing John's role.
4. *The logic of chapter 21 points directly to John.* The context of
   the fishing scene shows that the disciples present are Peter,
   Thomas, Nathanael, and the two sons of Zebedee. Peter is
   obviously not the beloved disciple, and there is no evidence
   or tradition that Thomas or Nathanael knew Jesus intimately
   or produced any Gospel. Of the sons of Zebedee, James was
   martyred early, according to Acts 12:2. This leaves John as
   the remaining possibility.

Is it possible to develop a profile of the author using indirect
evidence within the Gospel? As early as 1881 the famous New Testament scholar Westcott did just this and amassed impressive data
to defend the following arguments:

1. The author was a Jew.
2. The author was a Jew of Palestine.
3. The author was an eyewitness of what he describes.
4. The author was an apostle.
5. The author was the apostle John.

Most would agree with these steps, but many still might hesitate at point five. For Westcott, the link between the beloved disciple and the son of Zebedee seemed irrefutable. Westcott's colleague, J. B. Lightfoot, exhaustively asserted the same in an article in 1890 (published with lecture notes in 1893). It is doubtful the arguments presented by Lightfoot have ever been overturned.

We must remember that the question of authorship—especially when it comes to internal evidence—no longer turns on the discovery of *new* evidence. There is no new evidence; only a resifting of what has been known for years. And, as Lightfoot urged, no argument has ever been advanced to show the *impossibility* of the author being John the Apostle. Only an unwarranted skepticism would dismiss John's confident knowledge of Judaism and of Palestine.[7]

One major objection has always been that, if John had penned this Gospel, would he have referred to *himself* as "the disciple whom Jesus loved?" This is certainly a difficult question. But it loses its force when we recognize the possibility of *stages of authorship*. It is defensible to argue that the apostle John originated the historical traditions of the Gospel and that these may even have been written. These texts were treasured by his disciples, and when he died they took it upon themselves to organize and even edit them. This would explains the Gospel's final verses (21:20–24). By this account *the beloved disciple* became *a title of veneration* employed by John's disciples to revere their deceased leader.

External Evidence

It would be reasonable to ask if other Christian writers in the first or second centuries knew something about the Fourth Gospel. Such *external evidence* deserves examination as we sift the evidence for authorship. The rest of the New Testament does not point to the apostolic authorship of John, but then no New Testament books specifically mentions who wrote another specific book. Each writing stands on its own.

---

7. As does C. K. Barrett, *The Gospel According to St. John: An Introduction with Commentary and Notes on the Gospel Text*, 2d ed. (Philadelphia: Westminster, 1978), 119–23.

But the postapostolic era does provide clues.[8] While the Fourth Gospel was being read, debated, treasured, and in some cases discarded, the one constant affirmation was that the Gospel carried apostolic authority.

Most Christian literature written before 150 has disappeared. Of that which remains, numerous writings show Johannine influence. For instance, Ignatius, bishop of Antioch, who died at the beginning of the second century, alludes to the Fourth Gospel in two letters to Asian churches.[9] Polycarp's letter to Philippi is dated in this period and quotes 1 John (7.1). *The Shepherd of Hermas*, a late first-century work filled with mystical visions, often alludes to Paul—and to John. By 160 Melito of Sardis quotes the Gospel directly. Nunn notes that the late second-century writers Athenagoras of Athens, Theophilus of Antioch, Montanus, and Justin Martyr knew and used the Gospel. Not one of these leaders bothers to defend its authorship. Theophilus mentions a "John" as one of the authors of the New Testament but says no more.[10]

Not until Irenaeus is bishop of Lyons (c. 130–200) do we read a full explanation of the authorship of the Fourth Gospel. Portions of Irenaeus' works have been preserved by the fourth-century historian Eusebius' in *Ecclesiastical History*. Eusebius identifies John as the beloved disciple and a major leader in Asia (3.23).[11] Then he goes on to quote Irenaeus: "All the clergy who in Asia came in contact with John, the Lord's disciple, testify that John taught it [the Gospel? the truth?] to them; for he remained with them till Trajan's time."[12] Then Irenaeus is quoted to say that John lived in Ephesus—whose church "became a true witness of the apostolic tradition." Later Irenaeus is quoted by Eusebius to explain the origins of the Gospels. After describing the origins of Matthew, Mark,

---

8. See the thorough discussion in Henry P. V. Nunn, *The Authorship of the Fourth Gospel* (Eton, England: Alden and Blackwell, 1952); J. B. Lightfoot, "External Evidence for the Authenticity and Genuineness of St. John's Gospel," in J. B. Lightfoot, *Biblical Essays* (London: Macmillan, 1893; repr. ed., Grand Rapids: Baker, 1979): 45–122; and J. A. T. Robinson, *The Priority of John* (Yorktown Heights, N.Y.: Meyer-Stone, 1987), 36–122.

9. See the full study of Barrett, *John*, 110–11.

10. Nunn, *Authorship*, provides a full study and all of the original sources, 20–32.The study of Theophilus may be found in Daniel J. Theron, *Evidence of Tradition* (Grand Rapids: Baker, 1957; repr. ed., 1980), 73.

11. Eusebius *Ecclesiastical History* may be read in full in the Penguin Classics Edition, trans. G. A. Williamson (New York: Penguin, 1965).

12. Citation from Irenaeus *Against Heresies* 2.22.5. The full work survives in a fifth-century Latin translation of a much earlier work, possibly from the early third century.

and Luke, Irenaeus says, "Lastly John, the disciple of the Lord, *who had leaned back on his breast*,[13] once more set forth [or published, ἐξέδοκε] the Gospel while residing in Ephesus."[14]

So here we have an important witness from about 200 who says that the beloved disciple is John and that he was the source of the Fourth Gospel. But how can we be sure that Irenaeus knew what he was talking about? *What was the source of his testimony?* Irenaeus reports that his source was the bishop of Smyrna named Polycarp—and Polycarp was personally instructed by John. Polycarp was martyred in about 155 when he was 86 years old. This means that he was born in about 70, well within an age to have known John the apostle. In a popular translation listen to Irenaeus' own words about Polycarp:

> Polycarp was not only instructed by apostles and conversant with many who had seen the Lord, but was appointed by apostles to serve in Asia as Bishop of Smyrna. I myself saw him in my early years, for he lived a long time and was very old indeed when he laid down his life by a glorious and most splendid martyrdom. At all times he taught the things which he had learnt from the apostles, which the Church transmits, which alone are true. These facts are attested by all the churches of Asia and the successors of Polycarp to this day—and he was a much more trustworthy and dependable witness to the truth than Valentinus and Marcion and all other wrong-headed persons. In the time of Anicetus he stayed for a while in Rome, where he won over many from the camp of these heretics in the Church of God, proclaiming that the one and only truth he had received from the apostles was the truth transmitted by the Church. And there are people who heard him describe how John, the Lord's disciple, when at Ephesus went to take a bath, but seeing Cerinthus inside rushed out of the building without taking a bath, crying: "Let us get out of here, for fear the place falls in, now that Cerinthus, the enemy of the truth, is inside!" Polycarp himself on one occasion came face to face with Marcion, and when Marcion said "Don't you recognize me?" he replied: "I do indeed: I recognize the firstborn of Satan!" So careful were the apostles and their disciples to avoid even exchanging words with any falsifier of the truth, in obedience to the Pauline injunction: "If a man remains

---

13. Note the explicit connection with the Fourth Gospel (John 13:23) identifying John as the beloved disciple.
14. Irenaeus *Against Heresies* 3.1.1; Eusebius *Ecclesiastical History* 5.8.4.

heretical after more than one warning, have no more to do with
him, recognizing that a person of that type is a perverted sinner,
self-condemned.[15]

In another passage Irenaeus is writing to a friend in Rome
named Florinus, who is on the brink of heresy. Irenaeus here
explicitly states the *apostolic succession* of teaching of which they
are both heirs. He reminds Florinus how both of them sat in the
company of Polycarp and uses this to admonish Florinus about
his teaching.

> Such notions the elders of an earlier generation, those taught by the
> apostles themselves, did not transmit to you. When I was still a boy
> I saw you in Lower Asia in Polycarp's company, when you were
> cutting a fine figure at the imperial court and wanted to be in favour
> with him. I have a clearer recollection of events at that time than of
> recent happenings—what we learn in childhood develops along
> with the mind and becomes a part of it—so that I can describe the
> place where blessed Polycarp sat and talked, his goings out and
> comings in, the character of his life, his personal appearance, his
> addresses to crowded congregations. I remember how he spoke of
> his conversations with John and with the others who had seen the
> Lord; how he repeated their words from memory; and how the
> things that he had heard them say about the Lord, His miracles and
> His teaching, things that he had heard direct from the eye-witnesses
> of the Word of Life, were proclaimed by Polycarp in complete har-
> mony with Scripture. To these things I listened eagerly at that time,
> by the mercy of God shown to me, not committing them to writing
> but learning them by heart. By God's grace I constantly and consci-
> entiously meditate on them.[16]

To sum: Ireanaeus' authority stems from the succession through
Polycarp. John the apostle taught Polycarp; Polycarp taught Irenaeus. At about the same time as Irenaeus, the bishop of Ephesus
was a man named Polycrates. Polycrates wrote to Pope Victor I
(189–c 98), about controversies concerning Easter. Again the historian Eusebius has preserved a portion of the letter in which Polycrates links John with the beloved disciple and places him in Ephesus, as did Irenaeus:

---

15. Irenaeus *Against Heresies* 3.3.4; Eusebius, *Ecclesiastical History* 4.14.3–8. This translation
from edition cited above.
16. Irenaeus *Against Heresies* 2.22.5; Eusebius *Ecclesiastical History* 3.23.3–4.

In Asia great luminaries sleep who shall rise again on the last day, the day of the Lord's advent, when He is coming with glory from heaven and shall search out all His saints—such as Philip, one of the twelve apostles, who sleeps in Hierapolis with two of his daughters, who remained unmarried to the end of their days, while his other daughter lived in the Holy Spirit and rests in Ephesus. *Again there is John, who leant back on the Lord's breast, and who became a sacrificing priest wearing the mitre, a martyr and a teacher; he too sleeps in Ephesus.*[17]

By the end of second century there seemed to be a coming-together of ideas: The beloved disciple originated the Fourth Gospel; he was John the apostle, and he was associated with Ephesus. Justin Martyr (c. 100–165) resided in Ephesus in about 150 and speaks of John—one of the apostles—as having lived there. Ephesus has produced a third-century mausoleum in honor of John. The learned Tertullian of Carthage (160–215) assumes that this author is John, the son of Zebedee, when he defends the Gospel against heretics.[18] The same is true of Clement of Alexandria (c. 155–220) who gave John the famous honor of writing a "spiritual gospel."[19]

From this same period a peculiar document has survived in eighty-five lines of poorly translated Latin. The Muratorian Fragment (c. 180–200) is the most ancient catalogue of New Testament books and provides a sort of preface for the Gospels.[20] Lightfoot expressed confidence in it, attributed it to Hippolytus of Rome, a student of Irenaeus (c. 170–236), and pointed to a Greek original. The same respect is accorded it by modern scholars. Lines 9–34 give an account of John:

The fourth [book] of the Gospels is that of John [one] of the disciples. When his fellow-disciples and bishops urged [him], he said: "Fast together with me today for three days and, what shall be revealed to each, let us tell [it] to each other." On the same night it was revealed to Andrew, [one] of the Apostles, that, with all of them

---

17. Eusebius *History* 3.21.3 (cf. 5.24.2ff). Emphasis author's.
18. Tertullian *Prescription of Heretics* 22; *Against Marcion* 4.2.
19. Eusebius *Ecclesiastical History* 13.1.7.
20. The Latin text with notes is available in Brooke Foss Westcott, *The Canon of the New Testament* (London: Macmillan, 1881), 521–38 (compare with 211–20) and Theron, *Evidence*, 106–13. For E.T., see Edgar Hennecke, ed., *The New Testament Apocrypha*, 2 vols. (Louisville: Westminster-John Knox, 1963–1966), 1:42–45, or Henry S. Bettenson, ed., *Documents of the Christian Church*, 2d ed. (New York: Oxford University Press, 1963), 28–29.

reviewing [it], John should describe all things in his own name. And
so, although different beginnings might be taught in separate books
of the Gospels, nevertheless it makes no difference to the faith of
the believers, since all things in all [of them] are declared by the one
sovereign Spirit—concerning [his] nativity, concerning [his] passion, concerning [his] resurrection, concerning [his] walk with His
disciples, and concerning His double advent: the first in humility
when He was despised, which has been; the second in royal power,
glorious, which is to be. What marvel, therefore, if John so constantly brings forward particular [matters] also in his Epistles, saying of himself: "What we have seen with our eyes and have heard
with [our] ears and our hands have handled, these things we have
written to you." *For thus he declares that he was not only an eyewitness
and hearer, but also a writer of all the wonderful things of the Lord in
order.*[21]

A word of caution is in order. We have to employ these pref-
aces with some reserve since we cannot verify their authenticity.
Consider another Gospel preface. About forty copies of the Latin
Vulgate preserve the so-called "Anti Marcionite Prologues" to the
Gospels. Originally penned in Greek, all but Matthew has sur-
vived. What follows is the preface to the Fourth Gospel.

> The Gospel of John was manifested and given to the churches by
> John while still in the body, as Papias of Hierapolis, a dear disciple
> of John, has recorded in his exoteric, that is in his last five books.
> For he wrote the Gospel while John dictated standing (or accu-
> rately?). But Marcion the heretic, when he had been rejected by him
> because of his contrary opinions, was expelled by John. He had in
> fact brought writings or letters to him from the brothers who were in
> Pontus.[22]

Early scholars quickly offered this as second-century evidence.
But there are troublesome matters of detail: John could hardly have
personally rejected Marcion, and neither Eusebius nor Irenaeus

21. Translation from Theron, *Evidence*, 107–8. Emphasis author's.
22. For Latin, see A. Huck, *A Synopsis of the First Three Gospels* (Oxford England: Blackwell,
1935): v–vii. The Johannine prologue is omitted in the 1981 H. Greeven revision of Huck. E.T.
available in Richard G. Heard, "The Old Gospel Prologues," *Journal of Theological Studies* 6
(1955): 11; compare with Wilbert Francis Howard, "The Anti-Marcionite Prologues to the
Gospels," *Expository Times* 47 (1935–1936): 534–35; and Robert M. Grant, "The Oldest Gospel
Prologues," *Anglican Theological Review* 23 (1941): 231–32.

mention anything about John dictating to Papias. Thus many have rejected the prologue as historically worthless.[23] But the question is whether or not there is an historical nucleus behind it.

Much more could be added to this survey showing the extent to which the early church was confident in this Gospel's authorship. Origen, for instance, wrote the first commentary on John around 220 and never betrayed any knowledge that the Gospel's authenticity was in doubt. Of course by the early third century fictitious traditions could have become permanently embedded in the church to such a degree that these witnesses are unreliable. But the breadth and diversity of the tradition is surprising. Fictional narratives did exist—as witness in the fantastic apocryphal *Acts of John* and the Syriac *History of John*.[24] And by the fourth century these "historical" narratives could become very elaborate, as seen in Jerome.[25]

There have been objections to this external tradition which we have outlined:

First, the Fourth Gospel did experience opposition. Charismatic fringe groups emphasized the Spirit in John and gnostic theologians had fully embraced the Fourth Gospel. In reaction many church leaders rejected the Gospel itself. Christians without the Gospel were termed the *Alogoi* ("without the Logos"). Could a Gospel known to be from the pen of an apostle be so easily rejected? It is important to recall (as Brown reminds us) that these were fringe groups hardly representing mainstream Christianity.[26] They were considered heretics. And fringe groups in these centuries knew no limit to their claims (as in the case of Marcion). Some even attributed the authorship of John to the gnostic Cerinthus. We can reflect on the malice of this claim when we recall the story of John's disdain for Cerinthus in the Ephesian baths reported by Irenaeus (see above).

---

23. As do Heard, "Prologues," 16, and Bruce M. Metzger, *The Canon of the New Testament*, (New York: Oxford University Press, 1987), 94, n34. The dubious value is attributed to the *Latin Monarchian Prologues*, once hailed as second-century texts, but now dated to the fourth century or later.

24. See *Acts of John* in Hennecke, *Apocrypha*, 2:188–259. For E.T. of the *Syriac History of John*, see W. Wright, *Apocryphal Acts of the Apostles Edited from Syriac Manuscripts* (London: NP, 1871; repr. ed., Amsterdam: Philo, 1968): 2–60;

25. Jerome *Illustrious Men* 9.

26. Brown, *John*, 1:xcii; see also Nunn, *Authorship*, 71–86.

Second, another later tradition says that John was martyred with his brother James at a very early age. According to a ninth-century codex found in 1862, the ancient father Papias taught that John, the Son of Zebedee, was killed by the Jews.[27] This would mean that John never arrived in Ephesus and would jeopardize the traditional picture. These sources are very late, however, and find no support in other traditions. Further, the text says Papias was an eyewitness of John—but if John died early, Papias' involvement is remarkable. Today, this objection has fallen by the wayside.

Third, a more important objection, is the direct challenge of the words of Irenaeus. Irenaeus also claimed that Papias knew John, but the historian Eusebius promptly corrected him: Papias' own words show that he received the truth through elders and was *not an eyewitness to John. If Irenaeus was wrong about this, did he also fabricate the Polycarp story*? It is important to note that the discerning Eusebius does *not* amend Irenaeus' account of Polycarp. It is also significant that Irenaeus and not Papias claimed to know Polycarp personally.

Fourth, from a statement in Eusebius it appears that an *elder John* lived in Asia, a man different from the apostle John. Were these confused? Listen to the words of Papias given by Eusebius: "And whenever anyone came who had been a follower of the elders, I inquired into the words of the elders, what Andrew or Peter had said, or Philip or Thomas, or James, or *John* or Matthew or any other disciple of the Lord, and what Aristion and the *Elder John*, disciples of the Lord, were saying." Eusebius makes it perfectly clear so there is no confusion. Indeed, no ancient evidence promotes this other John as the author of the Fourth Gospel. *John Mark* mentioned in Acts 12:12 authored the second Gospel, as the Monarchian Prologue and Eusebius affirm. Papias may be referring to the same John twice[28] or simply indicating this other source of authority. At least to suggest a confusion in antiquity fails to make better sense of the external evidence we have already seen. At best it may explain Irenaeus' confusion about Papias, but little more.

27. Nunn, *Authorship*, 87–95
28. Stephen S. Smalley, *John: Evangelist and Interpreter* (Greenwood, S.C.: Attic, 1978), 73. The New Testament bears ample evidence that the apostles were elders (οἱ πρεσβύτεροι), such as 1 Pet. 5:1; 2 John 1:1. Papias himself even refers earlier to the first list as "elders."

Summary

By the time of Irenaeus the church with virtual unanimity ascribes authorship of the Gospel to the apostle. One could suggest that this was a very early tradition invented to defend the Gospel. In this case our sources cannot unravel the mystery. But this seems unlikely. The uniformity and breadth of support for traditional authorship makes it a fully defensible viewpoint. But in addition to this evidence must be added the internal evidence. The hypothesis that John the son of Zebedee is the beloved disciple—and the Gospel's eyewitness—fits well. At least there is no compelling evidence to overturn it.

Nevertheless we must be quite clear about what we mean by authorship. As we shall see, the Gospel shows signs of editing. And even though the apostle John was no doubt the fountainhead of the Gospel's traditions, its text was subsequently edited and reforged by disciples within the Johannine church.

Bibliography

Brown, Raymond E. *The Community of the Beloved Disciple.* New York: Paulist, 1979.

Bruns, J. Edgar. "The Confusion Between John and John Mark in Antiquity." *Scripture* 17 (1965): 23–26.

Cullmann, Oscar. *The Johannine Circle.* Philadelphia: Westminster, 1976.

de Jonge, Marinus. "The Beloved Disciple and the Date of John." In *Text and Interpretation: Studies in the New Testament Presented to Matthew Black.* Ernest Best and Robert McLaren Wilson, eds. New York: Cambridge University Press, 1979: 99–114.

Filson, Floyd V. "Who Was the Beloved Disciple?" *Journal of Biblical Literature* 68 (1949): 83–88.

Guthrie, Donald. *New Testament Introduction.* Downers Grove, Ill.: InterVarsity, 1970. See pages 241–71.

Lightfoot, J. B. "Internal Evidence for the Authenticity and Genuineness of St. John's Gospel" and "External Evidence for the Authenticity and Genuineness of St. John's Gospel." In J. B. Lightfoot. *Biblical Essays.* London: Macmillan, 1893. Repr. ed. Grand Rapids: Baker, 1979. 1–198.

Nunn, Henry P. V. *The Authorship of the Fourth Gospel.* Eton, England: Alden and Blackwell, 1952.

Parker, Pierson. "John and John Mark." *Journal of Biblical Literature* 79 (1960): 97–110.

_____. "John the Son of Zebedee and the Fourth Gospel." *Journal of Biblical Literature* 81 (1962): 35–43.

Robinson, J. A. T. *Redating the New Testament*. Philadelphia: Westminster, 1976. 254–311.

_____. *The Priority of John*. Yorktown Heights, N.Y.: Meyer-Stone, 1987. See pages 36–122.

Sanders, Joseph N. "St. John of Patmos." *New Testament Studies* 9 (1962–1963): 75–85.

_____. "Who Was the Disciple Whom Jesus Loved?" In Frank L. Cross, ed. *Studies in the Fourth Gospel*. London: Mowbray, 1957. 72–82.

Snape, H. C. "The Fourth Gospel, Ephesus and Alexandria." *Harvard Theological Review* 47 (1954) 1–14.

Wiles, Maurice F. *The Spiritual Gospel: The Fourth Gospel in the Early Church*. Cambridge, England: Cambridge University Press, 1960.

Part **2**

Literary Characteristics of the Fourth Gospel

3

How the Fourth
Gospel Was Built

In 1980, while I was a post-graduate student in the United Kingdom, I had the opportunity to meet the famous Johannine scholar, C. K. Barrett, at his office in Durham, England. With considerable trepidation I, as a young Ph.D. candidate, approached one whose commentary on the Greek text of John had been my tutor for years. I wanted to ask questions about matters that had come up in my research, and I desperately wanted to present myself with poise and confidence to show him that I had some grasp of Johannine scholarship . . . impress him, in other words! To talk "scholar to scholar" with Barrett had to be every fledgling Ph.D. candidate's dream. After a few moments of the usual niceties, Professor Barrett took the lead by asking me a few questions. His first volley: "Since you are researching the Fourth Gospel, Mr. Burge, perhaps you could explain the peculiar ending at 14:31." I well remember my thoughts as if it were yesterday: "14:31? What did 14:31 mean?" Things were definitely not going as planned.

Look at John 14:31. Note that Jesus has been in the upper room since chapter 13, no doubt celebrating his final Passover. At 14:31 he has ended his teaching and is dismissing the group. But then he goes on to talk to them for eighty-six more verses. Jesus does not finally leave Jerusalem and cross the Kidron Valley until 18:1!

What is going on here? Did Jesus stand outside the door from 15:1–17:26? Was he on the threshold of the upper room? Or, as Brooke Foss Westcott thought, did he teach and pray *enroute* to the

Kidron Valley, stopping perhaps at the Temple itself? Or have some chapters in John been switched around? Should chapter 14 immediately precede chapter 18? Note further in 16:5, how Jesus complains that no one has asked him, "Where are you going?" Now flip back to 13:36—*Peter had asked that very question.* Why does 16:5 follow 13:36?

It is time to look at the text of John directly. We are familiar with the history of its interpretation (chapter 1) and with the debate surrounding the origins and authorship of the Gospel (chapter 2). But these are background questions. Our primary aim now is to become adept at working within the text of the Gospel, to know its story and its literary peculiarities.

The challenge of 14:31 is only one case in point. Consider also John's first chapter. If I decided to teach or preach from John 1, I would have to make a decision about the native literary divisions of the chapter. Do I establish the sections as 1:1–18, 19–34, and 35–51? Further, I must ask about the connections between this chapter and the balance of the Gospel. Since the chapter divisions are artificial, it may be that themes spill from one chapter to the next. Read John 15:18–16:11. It is apparent that the theme of persecution in chapter 15 continues through 16:4a (a common paragraph break). The thematic unit must cross the chapter divide.

Exegesis, therefore, begins with a thorough knowledge of the text *as we have it.* It will not do to study a passage in isolation from its context. Nor will it do to neglect the wider theological framework of John and think that we can accurately discern the meaning of a particular narrative. This is an *ancient* text, a story almost two thousand years removed from us. It bears no copyright, no editorial history; we don't even possess an original first edition. Scribes hand-copied this Gospel for centuries—some of them were scrupulous and scholarly, others were, frankly, sloppy. So what is the condition of this story as it now sits in our hands? What is the *literary phenomenon* of the Fourth Gospel?

There is a voluminous scholarly literature of attempts to solve this Johannine mystery.[1] This is perhaps why Raymond E. Brown once remarked that Johannine scholars often enjoy detective stories in their leisure time.

---

1. Surveys of this literature are stunning in that they show the tremendous energy applied to the Fourth Gospel. Note these important works: E. Malatesta, *St. John's Gospel, 1920–1965*

We have a couple of assignments as we begin this task. First, can we learn something about how this Gospel was built? Does it betray any sources? What if the Fourth Gospel is really made up of a variety of editorial layers—perhaps collections of stories about Jesus and his miracles were combined with lengthy accounts of his teachings. If this is true and based on good evidence, then we will learn a great deal more about our text. Second, we need to stand back and look at the Gospel as a whole. In its present canonical form[2] can we discern a logic and symmetry? Does the Fourth Gospel possess an organizational structure that betrays its unity and theological message?

Literary Seams in the Fourth Gospel

Stephen S. Smalley reported in *Expository Times* that finding the literary origins and structure of John was one of the most pressing concerns in Johannine scholarship.[3] Puzzles seem to abound at every turn. Some, such as the literary critic, R. Alan Culpepper, have examined the whole of the Gospel and identified its rhetorical patterns.[4] Others have attempted to dissect the story of the Fourth Gospel into an arrangement of literary units to explore possible sources.

This puzzle of literary structure was the first critical issue recognized in the Gospel. As early as the second century, Tatian's Diatessaron rearranged major portions of John to fit the Synoptics. The process of textual dislocation must have been widespread. The Sinaitic Syriac version found in 1892 at St. Catherine's monastery in the Sinai desert of Egypt rearranged John 18 (the order of the Caiaphas-Annas interrogation) to "improve" the narrative.

What we seem to have are internal clues—perhaps we might

(Rome: Pontifical Biblical Institute, 1967); Gilbert Van Belle, *Johannine Bibliography 1966–1985: A Cumulative Bibliography on the Fourth Gospel* (Leuven, Belgium: Leuven University Press, 1988); Robert Kysar, *The Fourth Evangelist and His Gospel* (Minneapolis: Augsburg, 1975); John Ashton, ed., *The Interpretation of John* (Philadelphia: Fortress, 1986), and Gerald S. Sloyan, *What are They Saying about John?* (New York: Paulist, 1991). For current publications, skim *New Testament Abstracts* ("Fourth Gospel"), a summary of hundreds of books and articles of New Testament. research published three times each year. See chap. 6.

2. *Canonical* refers to the received literary form accepted in the church.

3. Stephen S. Smalley, "Keeping Up with Recent Studies: St. John," *Expository Times* 96 (1986): 102–8.

4. R. Alan Culpepper, *Anatomy of the Fourth Gospel: A Study in Literary Design* (Philadelphia: Fortress, 1983)

label them literary seams—which betray a history of composition. Unfortunately the solution to this problem is unlike that in the Synoptics where multiple traditions can be compared. For instance, if Matthew and Luke used Mark, their patterns of dependence and divergence might be analyzed. Some, of course have argued that John may have known the outline of Mark or a few of Luke's sections, but few would dare suggest direct literary dependence on the order of, say, Matthew's use of Mark. On the contrary, John's sources have left only subtle traces of their history.

Since John's sources are not "given away" scholars have developed techniques to unravel the Gospel's mysteries.[5] First, we might look for stylistic evidences of additional editorial hands. In Pentateuchal Criticism this has been attempted by tracing different forms of the divine name, resulting in the much-disputed Graf-Wellhausen source theory. In John we could note how λόγος (*word*) is employed in chapter 1 and then dropped. The same is true of crucial words like πλήρωμα (*fullness*) and χάρις (*grace*). The best studies have rejected this tool, however. The careful linguistic work of Eduard Schweizer and Eugene Ruckstuhl have fatally weakened source theories based on style and argue convincingly that the same hand was at work from chapters 1–21.[6] Note how an important word like δύναμις (*power*) is consistently replaced with a "Johannine vocabulary" for miracles: ἔργον (work) and σημεῖον (sign).

Second, we might look for ideological tendencies—passages in which rival points of view are represented. Some Old Testament scholars identify differing northern-southern kingdom attitudes toward the covenant and sacrifice in the Pentateuch. An author may use a source, yet consciously or unconsciously indicate disagreement with it. Where these disagreements are discernable, the source and its editor may be distinguished. No doubt Rudolf Bultmann was the expert at this sort of detective work in John. He catalogued numerous tendencies, such as interest in the beloved dis-

---

5. See Robert T. Fortna, *The Gospel of Signs: A Reconstruction of the Narrative Source Underlying the Fourth Gospel* (London, England: Cambridge University Press, 1970), 1–22, and idem, *The Fourth Gospel and Its Predecessors: From Narrative Source to Present Gospel* (Philadelphia: Fortress, 1988).

6. Eduard Schweizer, *Ego Emi. Die religionsgeschichtliche Herkunft und theologische Bedeutung der johanneischen Bildreden, Zugleich ein Beitrag zur Quellenfragan des vierten Evangeliums* (Göttingen: Vandenhoeck, 1938; 2d ed., 1965); Eugene Ruckstuhl, *Die literarische Einheit des Johannesevangeliums: Der gegenwärtige Stand der einschlägigen Forschungen* (Fribourg, Switzerland: St. Paul, 1951).

ciple, works vs. signs, and eschatology. Note how in 3:26 and in 4:1 narratives tell us that Jesus was providing water-baptism. Then, much to our surprise, in 4:2 the story is corrected to say that Jesus really did not baptize—only his followers did. Bultmann would urge that this reveals disagreement between author and source. But critics also have dealt harshly with this approach. D. Moody Smith and Robert T. Fortna question our ability to discern ideological strata.[7] Themes in John are too subtle, too nuanced. Besides, any author may employ a number of inner tensions. To assign one view to a more primitive level and another view to a redactor simply lacks objective evidence.

A third tool is more promising: We might look for contextual evidence. In Pentateuchal criticism some texts offer parallel or contrasting accounts (for example, the creation narrative) or there may be major literary rifts in the narrative. Surprisingly little has been done to exploit such evidence in John, though it is a distinguishing feature of John's literary puzzle.

Contextual Evidence In John

Contextual evidence comes in a variety of forms. Its purpose is to show some irregularity or narrative rift in the text. In *textual evidence* ancient manuscripts show discrepancies in the tradition. One Greek manuscript may record a paragraph or sentence one way, while another offers a different version. This is so, for example, in Mark's longer ending (16:9–20). Johannine texts vary only infrequently. The story of the adulteress (7:53–8:11) comes quickly to mind, but seldom do textual discrepancies bear a major significance for the interpretation of the Fourth Gospel (see 1:13, 18, 41; 3:34; 6:69; 14:3).[8]

One also may study the *parenthetical remarks* of the narrator-editor. These comments interrupt the story in order to assist the reader, and they imply that the author is using sources or traditions that

---

7. D. Moody Smith, *The Composition and Order of the Fourth Gospel: Bultmann's Literary Theory* (New Haven, Conn.: Yale University Press, 1965); Fortna, *Gospel of Signs*, and idem, *Fourth Gospel*.

8 For a study of the text of John, see Victor Salmon, *The Fourth Gospel: A History of the Textual Tradition of the Original Greek Gospel*, trans. M. J. O'Connell (Collegeville, Minn.: Liturgical, 1976). Commentaries on the Greek text of John generally point out specific text problems. See esp. C. K. Barrett, *The Gospel According to St. John: An Introduction with Commentary and Notes on the Gospel Text*, 2d ed. (Philadelphia: Westminster, 1978).

readers may not understand. These are frequent in John. In John 1:41 we are taught that the Aramaic name "Cephas" means Peter (or Πέτρος). In 19:31 we are told that the Jewish Sabbath is a "high day." In 4:9 Jewish-Samaritan tensions are footnoted ("for Jews have no dealings with Samaritans"). Occasionally John explains some awkwardness in the logic of the text. In 2:9 the steward of the wedding party may not have known the origin of the wine, but the narrator reminds us that the servants were genuine witnesses to the miracle. Other "reader helps" can be found in 4:2, where we are reminded that Jesus did not baptize anyone. But usually the narrator just assists the story, as in 6:1, when he says that the Sea of Galilee and the Sea of Tiberius are one and the same. This is where the source critic sits up. If John's reader understood "Sea of Tiberius" and if John wrote the entire narrative without sources, why didn't John use this phrase in the first place?

An intriguing set of parenthetical remarks explain an outlook that only came after Jesus was resurrected. In 2:22 the first-time reader learns that an enigmatic saying of Jesus about a "newly built three-day temple" really refers to the resurrection body. The narrator explains that everyone figured this out only after the resurrection. In 3:11 Jesus' monologue is suddenly interrupted by a sudden use of plurals. "We speak of what we know." Some have tried to argue that this is the Johannine community giving the play its chorus.

The third contextual tool identifies what I label *literary seams* in the text. In these instances the chronological, topical, or dramatic flow of the narrative appears disjointed. A well-known example of this in Paul is found in 2 Corinthians 6:14–7:1, a section that interrupts the logic of the apostle's argument. For this reason, it is sometimes explained as a fragment from another Pauline letter which is now lost.[9] John's Gospel abounds with these in a way that is completely different from the Synoptics.

These phenomena are so common that they have even received a technical name. In 1907 Eduard Schwartz coined the term *aporia* for these "difficulties."[10] This term has been taken up by Robert

---

9. This is by no means certain. Many scholars have argued eloquently that 2 Cor. 6:14–7:1 belongs right where it is and was not added later.

10. From the Greek ἀπορία (a difficult passing; cf. ἀπορέω, "to be at a loss") which described either an impassable maritime strait (ἄπορος) or in debate, a difficulty in logic. See Eduard

Fortna and Howard Teeple.[11] In English the earliest work on this problem followed Schwartz by three years and can be found in Warburton Lewis, *Disarrangements in the Fourth Gospel*.[12]

The Aporias in the Fourth Gospel

What are these aporias and how do they evidence "seams" in the Gospel's narrative?

1. Without the distinctive idiom and poetic style of the Johannine prologue (1:1–18) the Gospel would begin at 1:19 with John the Baptist and parallel the traditional Synoptic starting point. What is the origin of this poem? Who wrote it? What is its relation to the body of the Gospel?
2. Note how John uses the term "sign" for Jesus' miracles. In 2:11 and 4:54 these are numbered (the first and second "signs"); but the numbering system is not maintained and besides, many have asked, how can 4:54 be the second sign when 2:23 says that Jesus had done multiple signs earlier in Jerusalem?
3. Jesus "came into the land of Judea" in 3:22. The problem is that he has been in Judea since he attended a Passover feast in Jerusalem from 2:23–3:21.
4. A fascinating puzzle is the sequence of John 5 and 6. Jesus moves abruptly from Samaria to Galilee to Jerusalem back to Galilee again and back once more to Jerusalem, without transitions. In chapter 5 Jesus is engaged in a debate in Jerusalem. Now look at 6:1, "After this Jesus went to the other side of the Sea of Galilee." It is like reading a letter from a friend who has just described his vacation in Scotland salmon fishing. Then when you turn the page he says, "and after this, we crossed to the other side of Chicago." Surely, you say, something was left out.
   Compare this with what we gain just by reversing the order of chapters 5 and 6. Now 6:1 makes chronological

---

Schwartz, "*Aporien im vierten Evangelium*," in *Nachrichten von der Königlichen Gesellschaft der Wissenschaften zu Göttingen* (1907), 342–72; (1908), 115–88, 497–650.

11. Fortna, *Fourth Gospel*; Howard M. Teeple, *The Literary Origin of the Gospel of John* (Evanston, Ill.: Religion and Ethics Institute, 1974).

12. Cambridge, England: Cambridge University Press, 1910.

sense because Jesus finishes a miracle in Galilee at the close of chapter 4. Jesus then moves from the west bank of the sea to the east bank. Likewise, 7:1 currently follows chapter 6 only with difficulty: "After this Jesus went about in Galilee; he would not go about in Judea because the Jews sought to kill him." This concern for his life should be preceded by chapter 5 where in Judea the Jews elect to kill him. John 7:21–23 mentions "one deed" for which Jesus is persecuted, the healing of the lame man in chapter 5. Chapter 5 also interrupts some theological links between chapters 4 and 6, among them teachings about the water of life-bread of life; sign theology, and doing the work of God. This also harmonizes John's chronology with that of Mark, where events in Galilee are climaxed by the great feeding, and then the scene shifts to Judea. The new arrangement gathers up the Galilee stories into a unit (4, 6) before Jesus works in Judea (5, 7–11).

This rearrangement has its critics, including the commentaries of Barrett, C. H. Dodd, and D. A. Carson. There is an absence of manuscript evidence. This rearrangement also produces other tensions in the text. Carson believes moving the chapters would destroy a thematic unity they share as they stand. Such criticisms must be weighed against the solutions the theory offers. It is no accident that some scholars find this transposition compelling. Others wish to remain with the sequential problems as we have them. Either way the point is made: the text lacks a smoothness we have come to expect from a unified narrative.

5. In 7:3–5 Jesus is urged to reveal his signs in Judea, as if he had not yet been there, but in 2:23 and in chapter 5 he has already done so.
6. The story of the adulteress (7:53–8:11) interrupts the Tabernacles discourse but has theological connections with it. Here is a case where manuscript evidence is significant. This is probably a floating Gospel pericope which entered John (and Luke) late.[13]
7. An aporia could be noted at John 11:2. Here Mary of

13. Gary M. Burge "John 7:53–8:11: The Woman Caught in Adultery," *Journal of the Evangelical Theological Society* 27 (1984): 141–48.

Bethany is introduced as the woman who "anointed the Lord with ointment and wiped his feet with her hair." The only problem is that this anointing does not take place until the next chapter (chapter 12).

8. We have already noted the difficulty at 14:31. Here it appears that Jesus has completed his upper room discourse. He implies that his arrest is at hand by saying, "I will no longer talk much with you for the ruler of this world is coming" (14:30). Then he says, "Rise, let us go hence." The striking thing is that Jesus does have much to say—86 verses— before the coming of Judas. Should 14:31 be followed by 18:1? If read in this sequence the narrative flows with surprising ease.

9. Another aporia is found at 16:5, "None of you ask me 'Where are you going.'" On the contrary, Peter asked the identical question in 13:36 and Thomas in 14:5. This has inspired a host of rearrangement theories that try to place 16:5 before 13:36.

10. In 19:5, 9, 13 Pilate leads Jesus out of the praetorium twice in "order to present him to the Jews as their king," without ever mentioning Jesus reentering. In fact, when Pilate reenters the praetorium in 19:9 we are left wondering how he can speak with Jesus from verses 9–11 since Jesus was left in public view on the outside porch.

11. A better known difficulty comes in 20:30–31. Most scholars think this was the original ending to the Gospel: it offers a statement of purpose and some justification for the Gospel as a whole.

12. So what do we make of John 21? Did the author who wrote chapters 1–20 write this? Stylistically it is the same—21:14 even employs a numbering system for resurrection episodes that presupposes chapter 20. Equally important, the rivalry between Peter and John found in John 13 and 20 is replayed in chapter 21 when Jesus is sighted on the shore. But on the other hand a careful editor could have shaped the chapter to the style and format of 1–20. The most fascinating section is in the final two verses (21:24–25). Amazingly, here editors or writers different from the beloved disciple betray their identity, "This is the disciple . . . who has written these things, and we know that his testimony is

true." Is this first-hand evidence of John's disciples, who assisted him in editing the Gospel?

13. Equally fascinating is the origin of 21:25 about the lack of books to contain the story of Christ. The phrase "I suppose" is the only personal reference by the narrator. Manuscript scholia (marginal comments) as early as the eighth century suggest uncertainty about the verse. A substantial challenge is to decode Codex Sinaiticus on 21:25. The Gospel originally ended at verse 24 (a coronis or stylized letter marks the end). The scribe then scrubbed the vellum and added verse 25 with another coronis. Recently ultra-violet examination disclosed his changes. How do we explain the original omission of verse 25? Was it in the copy the scribe had on the desk before him?

This is a brief tour of some contextual seams or *aporias* which await the careful reader of the Fourth Gospel. Some scholars have assembled extensive lists of these. But discerning readers can usually come to the apostle John's defense, urging that *aporias* usually can be explained. It is the cumulative effect that is important. The supreme irony of the Johannine literary format is that—while many narratives show remarkable attention to detail and a concern for precision (especially chapters 9, 18, 19)—others appear rough and units of narrative seem to collide.

Assessment

To wrestle seriously with the text of John as we have it, we must come to terms with these contextual seams. Current explanations are that the author never finished the Gospel (Wilbert F. Howard; W. Grundmann), that the author produced two editions which have been artificially joined (Pierson Parker[14]), that John made later insertions and spoiled the original text, or that John wrote with disjointed stories (Rudolf Schnackenburg, Ernst Käsemann). William Wrede thought that John was a confused simpleton. Eduard Meyer suggested that he was clumsy. Walter Bauer thought that John just could not write. This at least is more charitable than Ernest Renan, who in 1867 chalked it up to John's increasing senility! The least

---

14. Pierson Parker, "Two Editions of John," *Journal of Biblical Literature* 75 (1956): 303–14.

likely possibility is that, subsequent to its completion, completed folio leaves were switched around. It is unlikely that John had a folio format because examples of folios from this time are quite rare. Further, attempts to compare the length of displaced sections with the length of one folio page have been unsuccessful.

Most recent critics posit a series of redactors or editors who compiled various diverse sources. Barrett feels these were written from traditions found in Mark. Dodd believes John's sources were oral, older than the Synoptics, and thus bearing a high degree of historicity. Sometimes, as in the case of Brown or Oscar Cullmann, this reworking of the Gospel is attributed to a "Johannine School" or a community of disciples of John who complied, organized, and edited their master's teachings.

Let's try to sum up the usefulness of this data for exegesis. What importance may we attribute to these literary seams?

First, most scholars think a consensus is nearing that the Fourth Gospel is made up of sources. The *aporias* betray the diverse historical traditions that make up the fabric of John. These seams are *positive objective data* and bear vital clues for us. The result is nothing new. Scholars from Bultmann to Smith have weighed the evidence for signs, narrative sources, and discourse sources all along.

Conservative exegetes may find that these results work to some advantage. Johannine source criticism may lead us in the same direction as the Synoptic problem. Rather than being the literary inventions of three prolific Christians, the Synoptics are well-crafted collections of ancient historical units, preserved by earliest Christendom. Now similar claims are possible for the Fourth Gospel. If John is using early traditions, his Gospel is hardly a late-first-century invention. On the contrary, it possesses striking antiquity and authenticity. Sources point to antiquity; antiquity points to authenticity.

The danger here is to say that uncovering earlier strata will lead to an earlier, more pristine message from John. This is, by the way, how Johannine form critics have eliminated such things as futurist eschatology and sacramental interest from John. D. Bruce Woll and Fernando F. Segovia have recently argued that the original core of the farewell discourse is found in 13:31–14:31 and all else is secondary.[15]

---

15. D. Bruce Woll, "The Departure of 'the Way': The First Farewell Discourse in the Gospel of John," *Journal of Biblical Literature* 99 (1980): 225–39; Ferdinand F. Segovia, "The Structure, Tendenz, and *Sitz im Leben* of John 13:31–14:31," *Journal of Biblical Literature* 104 (1985): 471–93.

But this neglects the overall literary and theological unity of John and makes the "garment serve the seams" rather than the other way around. Most recently Robert Fortna has published his attempt to locate the earliest stratum, the narrative source, which was subsequently edited by a redactor. And his premise is clear: the Fourth Gospel is like an old Victorian house whose grandeur and heritage will be seen only when the later efforts of painters and carpenters have been removed.[16]

Second, the recognition of *aporias* suggests that the process of writing, compiling, and editing the Fourth Gospel was more complex than we ever realized. Brown, for example, supports five separate stages of editing by a community, with various hands making their contribution at various times. All of this began, in my judgement, with John, the beloved disciple. The numerous reflexes to eyewitness testimony (19:35) must at least mean this. But it may be true that his community, his intimate followers, collated his teachings, organized them, and edited them. John 21:20–23 may even suggest that John had died.

Does 21:24 reveal the identity of a Johannine disciple? What does verse 24 mean when the writer says, "*we* know that *his* testimony is true?" Clearly other parties are buttressing the beloved disciple's report. If this is true, we may have ready evidence that editors substantially reshaped the text.

Complete rearrangement theories have not won the day, but Johannine *aporias* do affect our understanding of source criticism, authorship, and literary format. Authors still argue for reversing chapters 5 and 6. Nevertheless, very early in the process one hand obviously compiled the final edition, linking John's themes with uncanny theological power and conviction. Overarching literary unity can be seen in the delicate construction of plot/narrative (Alan R. Culpepper[17]), dramatic suspense (Stephen S. Smalley [18]), irony (Paul D. Duke [19]), or even forensic motifs (Allison A. Trites, Anthony E. Harvey[20]).

It is John's complexity, his mixing of elements, that troubles us.

---

16. Fortna, *Fourth Gospel*.
17. Culpepper, *Anatomy*.
18. Stephen S. Smalley, *John: Evangelist and Interpreter* (Greenwood, S.C.: Attic, 1978).
19. Paul D. Duke, *Irony in the Fourth Gospel* (Atlanta: John Knox, 1985).
20. Allison A. Trites, *The New Testament Concept of Witness* (New York: Cambridge University Press, 1977); Anthony E. Harvey, *Jesus on Trial: A Study in the Fourth Gospel* (Atlanta: John Knox, 1977).

In 1953 Dodd cleverly described the Fourth Gospel as a musical fugue: "A theme is introduced and developed up to a point; then a second theme is introduced and the two are interwoven; then a third and so on. A theme may be dropped, and later resumed and differently combined, in all manner of harmonious variations."[21]

Discourses and Miracles

If the seams in John imply a patchwork quilt, a combining of sources by some editor, then it should not surprise us to find that scholars have sought to look beneath the surface of the Gospel. Bultmann was the first to work out a thorough explanation of this Johannine *collage*.[22] He suggested that the Fourth Gospel originated with a *signs source*, a narrative of miracle stories and conflicts which may have ended with the passion narrative. Later an editor revised these stories and supplied the lengthy speeches or discourses of Jesus.

A Case Study from John 5:1–47

Let's look at a sample passage to see how this study works. Consider John 5:1–47. Note how the scene switches without warning from Jerusalem to Galilee, never completing the narrative at the pool of Bethesda. Could editorial comments have been added by a later author? Do they represent another later editorial layer? Jesus' monologue is listed in *italic*. For brevity only the beginning and end of this monologue is here included. Possible editorial remarks are in **bold**.

Some time later, Jesus went up to Jerusalem for a feast of the Jews. Now there is in Jerusalem near the Sheep Gate a pool, **which in Aramaic is called Bethesda** and which is surrounded by five covered colonnades. Here a great number of disabled people used to lie—blind, the lame, the paralyzed. One who was there had been

---

21. C. H. Dodd, *The Interpretation of the Fourth Gospel* (Cambridge, England: Cambridge University Press, 1953), 383.
22. See Rudolf Bultmann, *The Gospel of John: A Commentary*, trans. G. R. Beasley-Murray, ed. R. W. N. Hoare and J. K. Riches (Philadelphia: Westminster, 1971); see also Smith, *Composition and Order*.

an invalid for thirty-eight years. When Jesus saw him lying there and learned that he had been in this condition for a long time he asked him, "Do you want to get well?" "Sir," the invalid replied, "I have no one to help me into the pool when the water is stirred. While I am trying to get in, someone else goes down ahead of me." Then Jesus said to him, "Get up! Pick up your mat and walk." At once the man was cured; he picked up his mat and walked. **The day on which this took place was a Sabbath,** and so the Jews said to the man who had been healed, "It is the Sabbath; the law forbids you to carry your mat." But he replied, "The man who made me well said to me, 'Pick up your mat and walk.'"

So they asked him, "Who is this fellow who told you to pick it up and walk?" The man who was healed had no idea who it was, for Jesus had slipped away into the crowd that was there. Later Jesus found him at the temple and said to him, "See, you are well again. Stop sinning or something worse may happen to you." The man went away and told the Jews that it was Jesus who had made him well. **So, because Jesus was doing these things on the Sabbath, the Jews persecuted him.** Jesus said to them, "My father is always at his work to this very day, and I, too, am working." **For this reason the Jews tried all the harder to kill him; not only was he breaking the Sabbath, but he was even calling God his own Father, making himself equal with God.**

Jesus gave them this answer: *"I tell you the truth, the Son can do nothing by himself; he can do only what he sees his Father doing, because whatever the Father does the Son also does. For the Father loves the Son and shows him all he does. Yes, to your amazement he will show him even greater things than these. . . . "But do not think I will accuse you before the Father. Your accuser is Moses, on whom your hopes are set. If you believed Moses, you would believe me, for he wrote about me. But since you do not believe what he wrote, how are you going to believe me?"*

Some time after this, Jesus crossed to the far shore of the Sea of Galilee **(that is, the Sea of Tiberius)**, and a great crowd of people followed him. [NIV]

The scene opens with a crisp, quick-paced miracle story, much like we find in the Synoptics. The lame man is approached by Jesus, who heals him (5:1–9). Because it is the Sabbath Jerusalem's Jewish leaders confront Jesus and the man. Now watch what happens. The action halts after verse 15, where an editorial comment informs us that this is why they persecuted Jesus. Verses 16–18 lapse into sweeping theological generalizations, the line of narrative is lost, and then for 28 verses Jesus offers a densely rabbinic monologue (19–47) which is not woven into the story at all. Even 6:1 is no help! This chapter abruptly shifts from Jerusalem to Galilee without concluding the story.

What happened here? Have two sources come together? Was an ancient miracle story joined to a lengthy discourse at some point? This phenomenon appears throughout John. Discourses stand side-by-side miracle stories.

In 1988 Fortna published the most comprehensive study to date of this mystery.[23] In 314 pages of detective work Fortna tries to separate this ancient narrative source, sift out editorial comments, and reweave the theology of the original document. He even dates this source in the 40s or 50s and claims to be able to discern when the editor disagreed with the source.[24]

These efforts are common among Johannine scholars, but evangelicals have been reluctant to join in. Two reservations may be lodged, for understandable reasons. First, much of this spadework is entirely speculative. Fortna himself hopes that a mere 50 percent of it will find acceptance. Sometimes it is virtually impossible to reconstruct the literary history of a chapter. The chief problem is that, unlike the Synoptics, we have no other documents with which to compare John. We might be able to study the editorial efforts of Matthew by looking at Mark (a text Matthew may have known by some accounts). But the Fourth Gospel gives us nothing similar.

Second, Johannine scholarship is fascinated with the development of communities and faith. While this has academic interest, how can it assist the exegete to open up and understand the biblical text? In many of these studies the aim is to reconstruct the communities of Christians who stand behind the text and show how their faith changed and developed as new voices, hidden in the Gospel, struggled to be heard.[25] There is certainly value in understanding that early Christianity was dynamic. The Epistle of James

---

23. Fortna, *Fourth Gospel*.

24. For example, the source promotes the signs of Jesus as if they had merit for faith. Thus 2:11 says after the Cana miracle, "This, the first of his signs, Jesus did at Cana of Galilee, and he manifested his glory; and his disciples believed in him." Now compare the critique of "signs faith" in 4:48, 6:26 elsewhere. Apparently on later reflection the Johannine editor concluded that faith that possessed no "sign" had greater merit. Thus the affirmation is given to Thomas in 20:28, "Blessed are those who have not seen and yet believe."

25. Important examples of this can be found in Raymond E. Brown, *The Community of the Beloved Disciple* (New York: Paulist, 1979), and J. Louis Martyn, *History and Theology in the Fourth Gospel*, 2d ed. (Nashville: Abingdon, 1979).

may respond to a theological development that Jewish-Christians found troubling, and 1 John to the misuse of the Fourth Gospel's Christology and pneumatology.[26] Locating development of such trends within a single text, however, is dubious.

If we can say that the narrative source has greater antiquity, difficult interpretative questions follow: Is the narrative closer to Jesus and thus does it bear greater authority than the discourses? May editorial units be discarded or declared suspect at the will of the exegete? Consider John 4:1–3:

> The Pharisees heard that Jesus was gaining and baptizing more disciples than John, **although in fact it was not Jesus who baptized, but his disciples.** When the Lord heard of this, he left Judea and went back once more to Galilee. [NIV]

Do we toss out 4:2 since it clarifies Jesus' baptizing habits? Or is it evidence that Jesus did baptize (as 4:1 implies) but the editor wants to correct this?

Brown's Solution: Stages of Composition

Brown developed one of the best-known solutions to this literary mystery. In addition to his two-volume commentary on the Fourth Gospel, he published various articles[27] and in 1979 a volume, *The Community of the Beloved Disciple*, of his complete study.

Brown believes that the Gospel must be read on a variety of levels. He remarks in *The Community of the Beloved Disciple* that the Fourth Gospel "tells us the story of both Jesus and of the community. Primarily, the gospels tell us how an evangelist conceived of and presented Jesus to a Christian community. Secondarily, the Gospels reveal something about the pre-Gospel history of the evangelist's christological views. Thirdly, the gospels offer limited means for reconstructing the ministry and message of the historical Jesus."[28]

He attempts to chart the life of the Johannine church from its incep-

---

26. See the study of the dynamic and diverse New Testament community given by James D. G. Dunn, *Unity and Diversity in the New Testament: An Inquiry into the Character of Earliest Christianity* (Philadelphia: Westminster, 1977).

27. "Johannine Ecclesiology—the Community's Origins," *Interpretation* 31 (1977): 379–93; "'Other Sheep Not of This Fold:' The Johannine Perspective on Christian Diversity in the Late First Century," *Journal of Biblical Literature* 97 (1978): 5–22.

28. Brown, *Community*, 17; see the author's review in *Journal of the Evangelical Theological Society* 23 (1980): 167–68. See also Raymond E. Brown, "The Relationship to the Fourth Gospel Shared by the Author of First John and by His Opponents," in *Text and Interpretation: Studies in*

fig. 2

R. E. Brown's Five Literary Stages

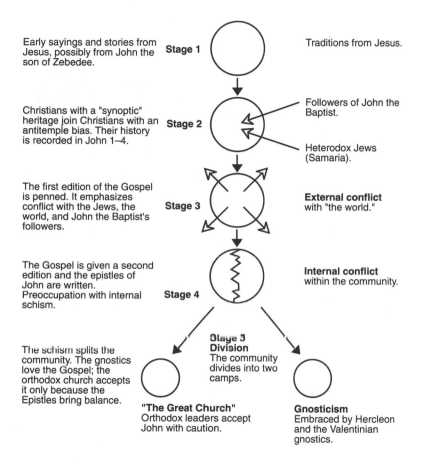

Early sayings and stories from Jesus, possibly from John the son of Zebedee. **Stage 1** — Traditions from Jesus.

Christians with a "synoptic" heritage join Christians with an antitemple bias. Their history is recorded in John 1–4. **Stage 2** — Followers of John the Baptist. — Heterodox Jews (Samaria).

The first edition of the Gospel is penned. It emphasizes conflict with the Jews, the world, and John the Baptist's followers. **Stage 3** — **External conflict** with "the world."

The Gospel is given a second edition and the epistles of John are written. Preoccupation with internal schism. **Stage 4** — **Internal conflict** within the community.

The schism splits the community. The gnostics love the Gospel; the orthodox church accepts it only because the Epistles bring balance.

Stage 5 Division
The community divides into two camps.

"The Great Church" Orthodox leaders accept John with caution.

Gnosticism Embraced by Hercleon and the Valentinian gnostics.

tion to its dissolution. This is the crucial new step. *Not only is the Fourth Gospel a window into the church, but it unveils a panorama of development.* The sequence of John's stories may be studied to unlock Johannine history. For Brown, this history consists of five phases (See Fig. 2).

During stage 1 a basic collection of Jesus' teachings circulates

the *New Testament Presented to Matthew Black*, ed. E. Best and R. M. Wilson (New York: Cambridge University Press, 1979): 57–68.

among Christians. Stage 2 dawns when two groups, one originating among followers of John the Baptist, the other among Samaritan Christians, merge; the resulting theology offers a high Christology and prejudice against the Jerusalem temple. Evidence of this comes from John 1–4. These convictions lead to the community's expulsion from the synagogue. In stage 3 the Gospel itself appears, and the community refines its structure and identity. Various struggles with the outside world ensue. Stage 4 finds the community torn by strife as fighting turns inward. Themes within the Gospel and the Johannine epistles reflect these themes. At stage 5 the community splits into two groups, one joining the "orthodox" church, the other entering the gnostic world.

Many scholars have been quick to criticize this reconstruction, but in fairness to Brown we note that he himself offers this schema only as a tentative theory. If only 60 percent of his ideas are right, he has said he will be satisfied. But for Brown this kind of sequence makes sense of the literary evidence

So we have a puzzle. The Fourth Gospel is a fractured text—seismic seams, literary lacunae, and editorial traces are abundantly evident. The phenomenon cannot be lightly dismissed, and interpreters must be aware of it as they move through the text. Awareness may help Bible students understand such rough passages as 14:31 and 16:5 and signs of textual tensions that suggest development.

But the exegete's task is best served when we study the text *as we have it.* A long tradition of commentaries represented by Rudolf Bultmann,[29] G. H. C. MacGregor,[30] and the section on John in Helmut Koester[31] (among many others) viewed exegesis as a dismantling and rebuilding exercise. But a new, infinitely more beneficial commentary seeks the theological message within the canonical form of the text. Such scholars as Brown,[32] Barrett,[33] Leon Morris,[34] George R. Beasley-Murray,[35] and others know the older tra-

29. Bultmann, *Gospel of John.*
30. G. H. C. MacGregor, *The Gospel of John* (Garden City, N.Y.: Doubleday, Doran, 1929).
31. Helmut Koester, *Introduction to the New Testament,* 2 vols. (Hawthorne, N.Y.: de Gruyter, 1987).
32. For example, *Community, and The Gospel and Epistles of John: A Concise Commentary* (Collegeville, Minn.: Liturgical, 1988).
33. Barrett, *Gospel According to St. John.*
34. Leon Morris, *The Gospel of John* (Grand Rapids: Eerdmans, 1970); idem, *Reflections on the Gospel of John* (Grand Rapids: Baker, 1986–1989); idem, *Jesus Is the Christ: Studies in the Theology of John* (Grand Rapids: Eerdmans, 1989).
35. John (Waco, Tex.: Word, 1987).

dition but choose for theological reasons to make sense of the Gospel as we have it—to explore its own coherence (instead of hidden strata) and to examine its final message (instead of traces of its development).

This brings us to an important next step. Can we discern a literary pattern in John? Does the present canonical text show an organization that might be useful for exegesis?

The Form of the Final Story

I often require students to photocopy the Fourth Gospel and make their own paste-up.[36] This enables them to see the Gospel in its entirety and note connections between units of text. John 11 (the raising of Lazarus) can now easily be compared with John 20 (the raising of Jesus). And thematic shifts can be marked with ease.[37] The abrupt shifts, say between John 5 and 6, become evident.

If we scan the entire Gospel we at once can see some natural divisions. All along, however, keep in mind that the chapter divisions in the Gospel are artificial. *We want to locate any natural literary divisions.* Jesus is at work in public from chapters 1–12, showing signs and teaching diverse audiences. From chapters 13–17 he speaks in private to his followers, almost saying "farewell" to them. The story ends with a detailed passion-resurrection account. We might illustrate the text as in Figure 3.

fig. 3
The Literary Divisions in the Fourth Gospel

1 12	13 21
Jesus' Public Ministry	*Jesus'Personal Glorification*

---

36. This is best done by photocopying a small devotional text with fine print, cutting apart the columns of text, and then pasting them in sequence on a large sheet of paper. The whole Gospel can now be viewed on a couple of sheets which students are fond of pasting to walls in their residence hall rooms!

37. An interesting first exercise is to highlight (with colored pen) every reference to a Jewish festival in the Gospel. You will find references to Sabbath, Passover, Tabernacles, and Rededication/Hannukah. Now note what stories are adjacent to these references. Is there a connection? Now use two different colors to highlight texts whose setting is in Judah and other texts whose setting is in Galilee. Do these colors show a pattern?

Let's look at the transitions between these units carefully. Chapter 12 seems a clear climax to the public ministry: it sums up Jesus' efforts, cries in despair over disbelief, and reaffirms the divine origins of Jesus' words. John 13:1 switches the scene to Passover, remarks that Jesus is now departing from the world, and narrows the stage to those who have followed him.

Chapter 17 ends a lengthy prayer and another geographical shift (the Kidron Valley) moves us to yet another scene, Jesus' arrest, trial, and death. *Lengthy discourses give way to dramatic narrative.*

Scholars have been quick to note these divisions and label them. Chapters 1–12 is called the "Book of Signs," since it records Jesus' numerous revelatory miracles. Chapters 13–21 (uniting the upper room and passion sections) is called the "Book of Glory," since on the cross Jesus is glorified (13:31).

The Book of Signs (John 1–12)

Look more closely at the first section, the Book of Signs. Note how the hymn at the beginning is almost an overture, a curtain-raiser to the drama, which really begins at 1:19. This is followed by a unit centered on John the Baptist and his disciples (and their earliest contacts with Jesus). The story moves quickly from scene to scene: a miracle at Cana; cleansing the temple; Nicodemus . . .

Sort these units according to theme, noting major narrative shifts. At once it becomes clear that these sections are *topically arranged*. From chapters 2–4 Jesus works miracles on institutions in Judaism; from chapters 5–10 he makes appearances at a series of Jewish festivals (note that each festival is named). In each of these—institutions and festivals—he replaces some Jewish symbol with messianic abundance (water becomes living water; manna becomes living bread . . .). We might venture an outline such as this:

    I. The prologue, 1:1–1:18

    II. Jesus and the Baptist, 1:19–51

    III. Jesus and the Jewish institutions, 2:1–4:54[38]
       A. At Cana, purification vessels, 2:1–12

---

38. In each case, the significant element in the Jewish institution is identified, and Jesus is seen replacing it with his own presence.

B. In Jerusalem, the temple, 2:13–25
C. In Jerusalem, a rabbi, 3:1–21
   (excursus on the Baptist, 3:22–35)[39]
D. In Samaria, a sacred well, 4:1–42
E. Return to Cana (close of the institutions section),
   4:43–54

IV. Jesus and Jewish festivals, 5:1–10:42[40]
A. Sabbath, 5:1–47
B. Passover, 6:1–71
C. Tabernacles (A festival of water and light), 7:1–52
   (excursus on an adulterous woman, 7:53–8:11)[41]
   1. A discourse on light, 8:12–30
   2. A conflict narrative on light and blindness, 9:1–41
D. Dedication (or Hannukah), 10:1–39
E. Return to the Baptist (close of the festival section),
   10:40–42

V. Foreshadowings of Jesus' death and resurrection,
   11:1–12:50
A. Lazarus: A paradigm of death and life, 11:1–57[42]
B. Jesus, anointed for death, enters Jerusalem to die,
   12:1–50

This could be visualized to underscore the structure of the story as in Figure 4, a schematic diagram highlighting principal parts of John 1–12.

Note how literary units are introduced by *internal* signals. Episodes in Cana (the first and second miracles) frame the section on Jewish institutions. The festivals are named, because in each scene Jesus does something to exploit a symbol of that festival in

---

39. Compare this unit with John 1:19–51. Many scholars think both sections originated from a similar setting.

40. As in the previous section, the festival is mentioned and its primary symbols described. Jesus then replaces the symbol or demonstrates his own authority over its meaning. At Tabernacles, when the temple was sponsoring water and light ceremonies, Jesus stands in the temple and announces that he is "living water" and "the light of the world."

41. This unit has been studied at great length and is no doubt foreign to this setting in John. Manuscript traditions are divided on its authenticity. See the author's study in *Journal of the Evangelical Theological Society* 27 (1984): 141–48, and the numerous references to studies listed there.

42. A careful comparison of this section and the passion story in chaps. 19–20 shows remarkable parallels.

fig. 4

The Book of Signs: John 1–12
"The Light shines in darkness . . ."

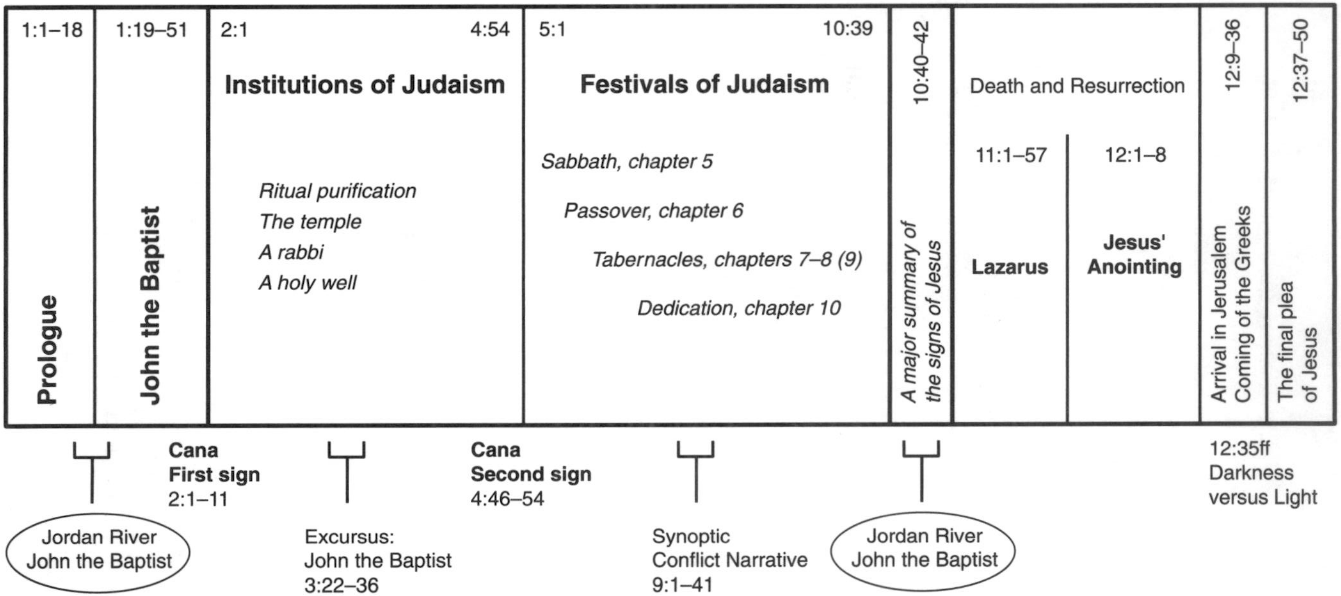

1:1–18	1:19–51	2:1	4:54	5:1	10:39	10:40–42	11:1–57	12:1–8	12:9–36	12:37–50
Prologue	**John the Baptist**	**Institutions of Judaism**		**Festivals of Judaism**		A major summary of the signs of Jesus	**Lazarus**	**Jesus' Anointing**	Arrival in Jerusalem / Coming of the Greeks	The final plea of Jesus
		Ritual purification / The temple / A rabbi / A holy well		Sabbath, chapter 5 / Passover, chapter 6 / Tabernacles, chapters 7–8 (9) / Dedication, chapter 10			Death and Resurrection			12:35ff Darkness versus Light

Cana First sign 2:1–11

Cana Second sign 4:46–54

Jordan River — John the Baptist

Excursus: John the Baptist 3:22–36

Synoptic Conflict Narrative 9:1–41

Jordan River — John the Baptist

his teaching (Sabbath-work, Passover-bread, Tabernacles-water and light, Dedication-Jesus' consecration). Generally he offers a discourse expanding the meaning of the symbols (see 6:15–35 as a comment on Passover). The final reference to John the Baptist (10:40–42) refers back to the beginning of the entire sequence of signs (1:19 and following), making another closing frame and reiterating the value of Jesus' signs. Finally, the closing two chapters serve as a sobering warning of what is to come.

Suddenly it appears that the Fourth Gospel may be topically arranged (at least in chaps. 1–12), even though the units or stories themselves have a clear historical and chronological character. John is telling us more about Jesus' messianic impact on Judaism than about the sequence of events in Jesus' ministry. The episodes are arranged by no accident. The John we possess has a careful, intentional organization.

The Book of Glory (John 13–21)

Much the same can be argued for the Book of Glory (chaps. 13–21). In this major section Jesus turns in private to his disciples during his final Passover. Remarkably, all nine chapters center on just a few days of Jesus' life. He teaches them privately about servanthood, washes their feet, explains the coming Holy Spirit in terms of personal revelation and persecution, and prays at length for his followers and their disciples. Chapter 18 opens the story of the trial and death of Jesus. As an extended narrative it reads much like the Synoptics, moving quickly from scene to scene without the characteristic Johannine discourses. The cross is followed by a detailed resurrection account in which Jesus anoints his followers with the Spirit. Finally, chapter 21 is likely an addition which adds resurrection stories in Galilee and Jesus' lengthy discussion with Peter.

We might venture an outline of Book of Signs as follows:

I. The Passover meal, 13:1–30
   A. The footwashing, 13:1–20
   B. The betrayal of Judas, 13:21–30

II. The farewell discourse, 13:31–17:26
   A. Jesus' departure and provision, 13:31–14:31

B. The true vine, 15:1–17
C. The disciples and the world, 15:18–16:33
  1. The enmity of the world, 15:18–16:4a
  2. Further Work of the Spirit, 16:4b–33
D. The priestly prayer of Jesus, 17:1–26
III. The suffering and death of Jesus, 18:1–19:42
  A. Arrest and interrogation, 18:1–19:16
    1. Arrest, 18:1–11
    2. The Jewish trial, 18:12–27
    3. The Roman trial, 18:28–19:16
  B. Crucifixion and burial, 19:17–37

IV. The resurrection, 20:1–29

V. Epilogue, 21:1–25
  A. The miracle of 153 fish, 21:1–14
  B. Jesus and Peter, 21:15–23
  C. Editorial appendix, 21:24–25

If we were to visually diagram the section, the result might be as in Figure 5.

The Book of Glory is dominated by the events of the upper room and the passion account. From chapters 13–17 Jesus is center stage, preparing his disciples for his death. Chapter 18 is a different sort of story. It seems the account of Jesus' trial and death was firmly established in early Christianity, perhaps by oral tradition. John 18–19 has more parallels with the Synoptic Gospels than any other section. This is why Dodd began with the passion narrative of John when he probed the Fourth Gospel's historical worth.[43] He concluded, though, that, while the Gospel echoes the Synoptics, its divergences were such that it probably recorded an ancient and authentic oral tradition about Jesus' death.

But what at first sight appears to be a smooth narrative shows on closer inspection to be a story assembled in much the same way

43. C. H. Dodd, *Historical Tradition in the Fourth Gospel* (Cambridge, England: Cambridge University Press, 1963), 21–151; F. F. Bruce, "The Trial of Jesus in the Fourth Gospel," in *Gospel Perspectives 1: Studies of History and Tradition in the Four Gospels*, ed. R. T. France and D. Wenham, (Sheffield, England: JSOT, 1980), 1:7–20; D. A. Carson, "Historical Tradition in the Fourth Gospel: After Dodd, What?" in *Gospel Perspectives II. Studies of History and Tradition in the Four Gospels*, ed. R. T. France and D. Wenham, (Sheffield, England: JSOT, 1981), 2:83–145.

fig. 5

The Book of Glory: John 13–21

"... and the darkness has not overcome it." John 1:5

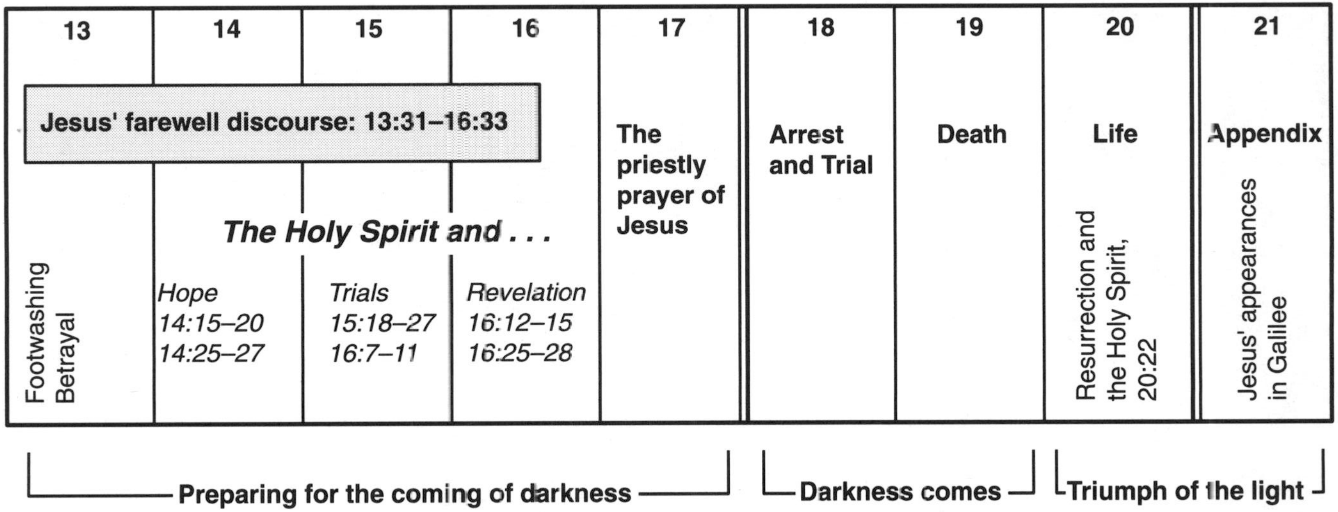

13	14	15	16	17	18	19	20	21
Footwashing Betrayal	Hope 14:15–20 14:25–27	Trials 15:18–27 16:7–11	Revelation 16:12–15 16:25–28	The priestly prayer of Jesus	Arrest and Trial	Death	Life Resurrection and the Holy Spirit, 20:22	Appendix Jesus' appearances in Galilee

Jesus' farewell discourse: 13:31–16:33

The Holy Spirit and . . .

└─────── Preparing for the coming of darkness ───────┘ └─ Darkness comes ─┘ └─ Triumph of the light ─┘

as the Book of Signs. Jesus' farewell (13:31–17:26) reads like a patchwork of teachings. We have already noted how 16:5 and the question of "going" follows 13:36 with difficulty. Commentators often
point out the many parallels between chapters 14 and 16, suggesting that we may have two renditions of similar materials. Nevertheless, the final edition combined these sources of tradition, organized them, and worked to give a coherent presentation of Jesus'
final days.

Conclusion

Clearly the text of John is made up of sources pieced together to
form a unified narrative. If we look carefully we can discern seams
where these sources have been stitched together. Some of them
are rough, rugged signs of an awkward assembly. But that is fine.
It shows us that John—no less than the Synoptics—is made up of
ancient sources that predate the authors' own efforts.

But this raises important questions. If John has been edited,
should we give a different worth, say, to the miracle stories than to
the discourses? If the editor was free to shape these narratives,
how much did he influence their final form? It is interesting to
remember that the language of 1 John is *exactly* like that of Jesus in
the Fourth Gospel. How much freedom did such editors have?

When we work with a passage in the Fourth Gospel, it is crucial
that we realize *where* in the longer text our passage comes from.
John's layout is not haphazard. If, say, we are discussing Jesus'
claim to be living bread (6:35), we *must* see the larger context in
the Book of Signs. Each theme is knit into the larger fabric and
when we pause to stand back, the garment we call the Fourth
Gospel takes on a striking and wonderful quality.

Bibliography

Brown, Raymond E. *The Community of the Beloved Disciple*. New York:
    Paulist, 1979.
Carson, D. A. "Current Source Criticism of the Fourth Gospel. Some
    Methodological Questions." *Journal of Biblical Literature* 97 (1978):
    411–29.

Culpepper, R. Alan. *The Anatomy of the Fourth Gospel: A Study in Literary Design*. Philadelphia: Fortress, 1983.

Dodd, C. H. *Historical Tradition in the Fourth Gospel*. Cambridge, England: Cambridge University Press, 1963.

Ellis, Peter F. *The Genius of John: A Composition-Critical Commentary on the Fourth Gospel*. Collegeville, Minn.: Liturgical, 1984.

Fortna, Robert T. *The Fourth Gospel and Its Predecessor: From Narrative Source to Present Gospel*. Philadelphia: Fortress, 1988.

_____. *The Gospel of Signs: A Reconstruction of the Narrative Source Underlying the Fourth Gospel*. London: Cambridge University Press, 1970.

Kysar, Robert. *John: The Maverick Gospel*. Atlanta: John Knox, 1976.

Smith, D. Moody. *The Composition and Order of the Fourth Gospel: Bultmann's Literary Theory*. New Haven, Conn.: Yale University Press, 1970.

Robinson, J. A. T. *The Priority of John*. Yorktown Heights, N.Y.: Meyer-Stone, 1985.

Teeple, Howard M. *The Literary Origin of the Gospel of John*. Evanston, Ill.: Religion and Ethics Institute, 1974.

Part **3**

A Strategy for Exegesis of the Fourth Gospel

Introduction to Part 3

The rough draft of your exegesis paper is due on Friday, but on Tuesday afternoon the project remains "on hold." Knowing how to start wins half the battle. The third floor of the library seems to be a maze of commentaries, lexicons, journals, files, and obscure books. Computers stand at ready for sophisticated bibliographic searches. Fantastic resources lie all about, but to the novice researcher their riches lie buried beneath sheer volume and variety.

Armed with a cursory knowledge of the history of Johannine literature (chap. 1) and a familiarity with the origins and authorship of the Fourth Gospel (chap. 2), we introduced the literary patterns within the text (chap. 3). Ahead lies the task of developing a strategy for interpreting specific texts—a game plan aware of critical issues and responsive to the original cultural and historical setting. Above all our exegetical strategy must unveil John's rich theological message.[1]

Exegesis is derived from ἐξάγω (*exagō*), a Greek word meaning "to lead out." Interpreters of Scripture employ this technical term because they want to *lead out* original meaning from the text—by no means an easy task! The text of the Fourth Gospel stands almost

---

1. Other strategies to exegesis and helpful background information are provided in: Otto Kaiser and Werner G. Kümmel, *Exegetical Method, A Student's Handbook*, rev. ed., trans. E.V.N. Goetschius and M. J. O'Connell (New York: Seabury, 1981); Gordon D. Fee, *New Testament Exegesis. A Handbook for Pastors and Teachers* (Philadelphia: Westminster, 1983); I. Howard Marshall, ed., *New Testament Interpretation, Essays on Principles and Methods* (Grand Rapids: Eerdmans, 1977); D. A. Carson, *Exegetical Fallacies* (Grand Rapids: Baker, 1984); and the Guides to New Testament Exegesis series, which includes this volume; Scot McKnight, *Interpreting the Synoptic Gospels* (Grand Rapids: Baker, 1988); Scot McKnight, ed., *Introducing New Testament Interpretation* (Grand Rapids: Baker, 1989), and J. Ramsey Michaels, *Interpreting the Book of Revelation* (Grand Rapids: Baker, 1992).

two thousand years removed from our world. Already we have seen a few of the literary puzzles that obscure the Fourth Gospel; even without such obstacles, some passages are difficult to understand. Often the story presumes that we know historical or geographical details, as when 4:20 records the woman of Samaria saying, "Our ancestors worshipped on this mountain; and you say in Jerusalem is the place that people ought to worship." Which mountain does she mean? Why is it important? In 7:37 Jesus speaks at length in the temple about thirst, water, and the Spirit *on the final day of the Feast of Tabernacles*. Does this festival somehow merge these themes?

Other passages bear a uniquely Johannine (or some might say, a "uniquely cryptic") message. Consider 6:63, "It is the Spirit that gives life, the flesh is of no avail." . . . or 1:14, "And the word became flesh and dwelt among us, full of grace and truth, and we have beheld his glory." . . . or 20:22, "And Jesus breathed on them and said, 'Receive the Holy Spirit.'" Can we unravel such symbolic and theological intricacy? If Peter regarded some of Paul's writings as difficult to understand (2 Pet. 3:16), no doubt the same could be said about John.

Five specific steps comprise the most effective strategy. In chapters 4–9 we shall examine each of them carefully. A simplified outline of these necessary steps would look like this:

1. Examine the *original text* of the passage.
2. Examine the *literary context* and *pattern of thought* in the passage.
3. Examine the *best academic studies* on the passage.
4. Examine the *cultural context* of the passage.
5. Examine *how John uses words*. Examine what makes the Johannine vocabulary unique.

First a word of caution. It is tempting to move directly to well–known commentaries for an explanation of a passage without doing the preliminary homework. While these works are valuable, they depend on the research of the scholar who produced them. The result may be uneven. For instance, students often find and use Merrill C. Tenney's commentary, *John, The Gospel of Belief*.[2] Yet

---

2. Grand Rapids: Eerdmans, 1948.

the author studies John 7:37–39[3] without mentioning a major punctuation problem in verse 37. How we punctuate these verses greatly influences our interpretation of the passage.

Similarly, Rudolf Bultmann's important critical work, *The Gospel of John: A Commentary*[4] explains the miracle of turning water into wine in John 2 as a spin-off from the Greek Dionysus legend.[5] Few scholars today take that approach, yet I have read many student papers which cite this myth as the key to the text. The problem does not pertain only to older books. Kenneth Grayston's recent commentary, *The Gospel of John*,[6] refers to Jesus' shepherd metaphor in John 10 without a careful comparison of Jerusalem's Hannukah themes and Jesus' use of the festival in his message.[7] Such deficiencies can be found by skimming any major commentary. Each of these books reflects the industry and interests of the scholar who produced it.

Careful exegesis, then, depends on personal labors in addition to the efforts of others. Each of the five steps listed above will be discussed in detail in part 3. They may be summarized:

1. Examine the *original text* of the passage (chapter 4). Having chosen a text for study, we begin with basic *textual–grammatical criticism*. This study verifies the Greek text and notes any manuscript discrepancies, including such matters as how to punctuate the Greek sentences.

2. Examine the *literary context* and *pattern of thought* in the passage (chap. 5). In *literary criticism* of the passage we learn as much as we can about the literary structure of the text. What is its flow of thought? How does it relate to surrounding material? What are its internal building blocks? This inquiry requires three studies: (1) a comparison of the Johannine passage with the wider New Testament context and, in particular, with the Synoptics (Mattthew, Mark, and Luke); (2) a comparison with the overall Gospel so we can see how the passage fits within John's literary schema, and (3) a study of the passage's internal literary structure.

3. Ibid., 134–37.

4. 1964; E.T., Philadelphia: Westminster, 1971.

5. Ibid., 117–21.

6. Philadelphia: Trinity, 1991.

7. Ibid., 83–89.

3. Examine the *best academic studies* on the passage (chap. 6). We must build a bibliography. While we don't depend on secondary sources entirely, others have gone before us, and we should benefit from their labors, using abstracts, monographs, and even computers. The appendix catalogs commentaries standard to any exegetical work on the Fourth Gospel.

4. Examine the *cultural context* of the passage (chap. 7). Metaphors, ideas, and assumptions advance the story. Understanding may require a knowledge of Jewish festivals (as in John chaps. 6 and 7), or it may require that we look into behavior that is foreign to us (such as shepherding in John 10 or footwashing in John 13). We may even need to review first–century history.

5. Examine *how John uses words* (chaps. 8 and 9). Every passage naturally consists of words. Syntax connects these smallest components of communication to other words, sentences, and paragraphs. We must ask, "How does the Gospel of John use its words?" Answering this question for a particular passage means: (1) doing a comparative lexical study using reference tools and computers, and (2) applying tools that help interpret John's words in a broad biblical and extrabiblical context.

Exegesis does not stop after completing the five steps. We need to distill John's message from our research and pursue two more steps to decide what John was saying in his own historical context—and to explain what John means for us in our context. Thus, we can expand our list to take in the logical conclusion of the exegetical process:

6. Examine what John communicated to his original readers.

7. Examine what John says to us today.

This last goal is crucial for those who are ministers of the Word of God. Once we have studied the grammar, history, culture, and language of the Fourth Gospel and come to some conclusion about the Gospel's historic message, *we must go further to discover how this message speaks with power, authority, and authenticity.* This will be our concern in part 4, chapters 11 and 12.

4

The Text

Since the original manuscript of the Fourth Gospel was penned in Greek[1], it is necessary for us to know the condition of this ancient text that manuscript study has given to us. Literally hundreds of copies of the Fourth Gospel have been preserved from the earliest centuries of the church. Because they were copied by hand, each bears its own peculiar set of distinguishing textual features. These alternative readings of a verse or word are called textual variants, that is, they are variations in how the text reads from manuscript to manuscript. Gaining access to this information, however, becomes a problem for university students and many seminary students who do not know Greek. Even students who have completed a year of Greek find the critical apparatuses bewildering.

But this process is important. Even in this century valuable papyrus manuscripts of the Fourth Gospel from A.D. 200 have been discovered and published. For instance, p^{66} (so indicated because it is designated papyrus number 66) was published in 1956, giving us almost all of John 1–14. Manuscript p^{75} was published in 1961 and contains John 1–12 and fragments of chapters 13–15. The textual history of the Gospels is complicated, but understanding it is, in some cases, an essential discipline. Consider John 1:18:

---

1. Although some scholars have argued at length that John was originally written in Aram. and translated into Gk., the earliest copies we possess are Gk. See Matthew Black, *An Aramaic Approach to the Gospels and Acts*, 3d ed. (Oxford, England: Clarendon, 1967).

No one has ever seen God; the *only Son*, who is in the bosom of the
Father, he has made him known. [RSV]

An important—critically important—set of ancient manuscripts
describe Jesus not as "the Son" but as "God"! The NIV follows this
reading, translating 1:18:

No one has ever seen God, but *God the One and Only*, who is at the
Father's side, has made him known.

The NRSV takes another approach:

No one has ever seen God. It is God the only Son, who is close to
the Father's heart, who has made him known.

Is 1:18 a high claim describing Jesus as God the only revealer of
the Father? Manuscripts p^{66} and p^{75} give no reference to "son," yet
a decision must be made concerning the interpretation of the text.

Small variants can have theological implications, as in 14:17:
"for he [the Spirit] *abides* with you and *will be* in you." Greek manuscripts give a variety of options for these tenses (present + future;
future + future; present + present). Is the Holy Spirit now *with* the
disciples and *in them* in the future? Or with them *and* in them in
the future?

If you know Greek

Exegetes with a working knowledge of Greek must use a critical
edition of the Greek New Testament. They should become familiar
with two editions:

United Bible Society, *The Greek New Testament*, 3d ed., ed. Kurt Aland et
al. (New York: UBS, 1975). The standard abbreviation used to refer
to this work is UBS[3].
Eberhard Nestle and Kurt Aland. *Novum Testamentum Graece*, 26th ed.
(Stuttgart, Germany: Deutsche Bibelstiftung, 1979). The standard
abbreviation is NA[26].

UBS[3] tends to show fewer variant readings and provides more
textual witnesses for each variant. It has one interesting feature.
Since the editors must make a choice of which variant their own

edition incorporates, UBS[3] footnotes rate the editors' confidence in the rendering they have used—from a high *A* probability to a doubtful *D* probability.[2] Although most students find this volume easier to use (its text is larger and its apparatus more simple), the NA[26] is often the choice of scholars because it offers so many more readings.[3] For instance, in John 7:52 the UBS[3] fails to mention that some important manuscripts (p^{66} and p^{75}) include the definite article with "prophet," making the verse say something completely different.[4] The NA[26] critical notes are more difficult to use, but a helpful introduction (pp. 39–72) makes it something any student can master.

These Greek texts identify variants in the passage. But sometimes difficulties arise just in reading the text or in discerning why scribes may have made the improvements they did. Help with the Greek may be needed. In such cases two volumes are indispensable:

Fritz Rienecker, trans. *Linguistic Key to the Greek New Testament*, ed. Cleon L. Rogers, Jr. (Grand Rapids: Zondervan, 1980).

Max Zerwick. *A Grammatical Analysis of the Greek New Testament*, 2 vols. (Rome: Biblical Institute, 1974, 1979).

The *Linguistic Key* primarily helps analyze or *parse*[5] words in a sentence. The *Grammatical Analysis* is better, since it not only parses difficult words but also translates almost all of them and gives a thorough explanation of difficult grammatical forms and idioms. Both based on the UBS[3], these two volumes are indispensable to the language study of any exegete.

---

2. See the helpful volume by Bruce M. Metzger, in cooperation with the United Bible Societies editorial committee, *A Textual Commentary on the Greek New Testament* (New York: UBS, 1971), in which all decisions for UBS[3] are explained. This is a vitally important volume every student of the Gk. New Testament should possess.

3. For an urgent defense of this text as the only real alternative, see Scot McKnight, *Interpreting the Synoptic Gospels* (Grand Rapids: Baker, 1988), 47–50. McKnight believes that the NA[26] provides almost twenty times more references. He also notes the advantage that the NA[26] is the basis for the Aland *Synopsis* of the Gospels (see below). For a critical comparison of the two texts, see Barbara Aland and Kurt Aland, *The Text of the New Testament*, trans. E. F. Rhodes (Grand Rapids: Eerdmans, 1987), 218–62. However we must be clear that even the NA[26] omits many text variants and the additional ones it includes (omitted in the UBS[3]) are often less crucial than we think in exegesis.

4 UBS[3] reads: "search and see that *a* prophet will not arise in Galilee;" the NA[26] shows this variant: "search and see that *the* prophet will not arise in Galilee."

5. *Parsing* means to note the gender, number, and case of nouns, or the tense, voice, and mood of verbs.

If you don't know Greek

Just one look at a critical edition of the Greek New Testament is enough to fill many students with despair. The page itself appears to have more in common with calculus than with the Bible. Nevertheless it is still possible to gain some information about the original condition of the text we are studying.

Begin by looking in a commentary devoted to the Greek text of the gospel. Particularly excellent are commentaries of John Henry Bernard,[6] Rudolf Schnackenburg,[7] C. K. Barrett,[8] Ernst Haenchen,[9] and George R. Beasley-Murray.[10] Barrett and Schnackenburg assume readers can move through the Greek text with ease and therefore may be difficult (though not impossible) to follow. Beasley-Murray offers an English translation with superscript footnotes, which are explained in a section. If there are significant variants in the text, these scholars are sure to note them.

In addition, technical commentaries based on the English text of the Gospel will likewise note variants. For instance, Raymond E. Brown's two-volume commentary[11] discusses a section of the Gospel, first by giving a new translation and second by "Notes." Brown's notes are technical, interpretative comments on the text and are filled with important variants. The same is true of Leon Morris[12] and Joseph N. Sanders and B. A. Mastin[13] (see footnotes) and, to a lesser extent, Barnabas Lindars.[14] By no means should a student read a couple of English-text commentaries, find no references to textual discrepancies, and assume there are no crucial variants. Many commentators omit this information, thinking it of minimal interest to the reader.[15]

---

6. *A Critical and Exegetical Commentary on the Gospel of John*, 2 vols., ed. A. H. McNeile (New York: Scribner's Sons, 1929).

7. *The Gospel According to St. John*, 3 vols. (New York: Crossroad, 1980–1982).

8. *The Gospel According to St. John: An Introduction with Commentary and Notes on the Gospel Text*, 2d ed. (Philadelphia: Westminster, 1978).

9. *The Gospel of John*, 2 vols., trans. R. W. Funk (Philadelphia: Fortress, 1984).

10. *John* (Waco, Texas: Word, 1987).

11. *The Gospel According to John*, 2 vols. (New York: Doubleday, 1977).

12. *Gospel of John* (Grand Rapids: Eerdmans, 1970).

13. *The Gospel According to St. John* (Peabody, Mass.: Hendrickson, 1987).

14. *The Gospel of John* (London: Oliphants, 1972).

15. The best solution for one who does not know Gk. would be to ask a seminarian, a professor, or a Gk. student for help. Generally the nature of text variants will become evident quickly to one who studies the language.

Determining Types of Manuscript Variants

What kind of variations or discrepancies are we looking for? What sort of variants need to be recognized? Generally, three situations present themselves:

First, a significant portion of the text may have a questionable place in the Gospel. This may pertain to whole passages, verses, or even words. For example, John 7:53–8:11 (the woman caught in adultery) has a remarkable and complicated text history. In many manuscripts it does not even appear; therefore, we need to ask, "Is this story itself original to the Fourth Gospel?"[16] This assumption must be carefully distinguished from discussions in commentaries suggesting that such passages as John 21 are not original to the text. In many of these cases there is absolutely no manuscript evidence for such an assertion. It is simply the hypothesis or suggestion of the author or other scholars.

Second, there may be linguistic variations in the text, such as changes in word order or selection. Many times these differences are insignificant and can be attributed to scribal attempts to "improve" the language of the Greek. But at other times differences cannot be explained so easily. Some decision must be made concerning the origin of the variant. Look at John 1:34, where John the Baptist testifies at the baptism of Jesus, "I have seen and I have testified that this is *the son* of God." Curiously, a handful of ancient manuscripts, among them the ancient Syriac, the old Latin, and the original hand of Codex Sinaiticus, read, *"the chosen one* of God." It is easy to see why a scribe might introduce the change from *chosen* to *son*, since this would sharpen the Christology of the Gospel, but the reverse makes less sense. *Chosen of God* is what we call the *more difficult reading,* and often it is the right one. Is *chosen* the original reading?[17] Such decisions must play a role in exegesis.

---

16. For a typical study of the history of this manuscript problem, see Gary M. Burge, "John 7:53–8:11. The Woman Caught In Adultery," *Journal of the Evangelical Theological Society* 27 (1977): 31–45.

17. Some scholars would say "Yes." The story of the baptism in John emphasizes Jesus' anointing in the Spirit and is likely echoing Isaiah 42 which unites the themes of Spirit, anointing, and election (not sonship). See the commentary remarks of Rudolf Schnackenburg and a more specialized study in Gary M. Burge, *The Anointed Community, The Holy Spirit in the Johannine Tradition* (Grand Rapids: Eerdmans, 1987), 59–61.

Third, we have to keep in mind that the original Greek manuscripts did not employ punctuation as we know it. Later manuscripts use full and partial stops (periods and commas, for example) but these are scribal decisions, which may or may not reflect the original intention of the passage. Consider for example the punctuation of John 7:37–38 in the Jerusalem Bible and the New International Version:

> On the last and greatest day of the festival, Jesus stood there and cried out:
> "If any man is thirsty, let him come to me!
> Let the man come and drink who believes in me!"
> As the scripture says: From his breast shall flow fountains of living water. [JB]

> On the last and greatest day of the Feast, Jesus stood and said in a loud voice,
> "If anyone is thirsty, let him come to me and drink.
> Whoever believes in me,
> as the Scripture has said, streams of living water will flow from within him." [NIV]

The same text in Greek appears as follows:

Ἐν δὲ τῇ ἐσχάτῃ ἡμέρᾳ τῇ μεγάλῃ τῆς ἑορτῆς
εἰστήκει ὁ Ἰησοῦς καὶ ἔκραξεν λέγων,
Ἐάν τις διψᾷ ἐρχέσθω πρός με καὶ πινέτω.
ὁ πιστεύων εἰς ἐμέ, καθὼς εἶπεν ἡ γραφή,
ποταμοὶ ἐκ τῆς κοιλίας αὐτοῦ ῥεύσουσιν ὕδατος ζῶντος.

The most obvious difference is that the Jerusalem Bible does not attribute the scripture citation to Jesus while the New International Version does. But a more careful look shows something else. Note that the JB suggests that the believer is not the source of the fountains of living water, but rather, the believer is urged to come to Jesus and drink. Jesus is the fountain. Now look at the NIV. Here the verbs and participles are organized in such a manner that the *believer* is identified as the one in whom streams of living water will be found. Both versions are defensible translations of the Greek grammar and the decision is strictly editorial. Does a full stop precede "as the scripture says" (JB) or should the participle "whoever believes in me" become a part of the citation (NIV)?[18]

Another interesting rendering of John 7:37–38 is the recently published New Revised Standard Version. Keeping in mind the interpretative problem with these verses, note how this text supplies a completely unwarranted adjective "out of the *believer's* heart" in verse 38:

> On the last day of the festival, the great day, while Jesus was standing there, he cried out:
> "Let anyone who is thirsty come to me,
> and let the one who believes in me drink,"
> As the scripture has said, "Out of the **believer's** **heart** shall flow rivers of living water." [NRSV]

Be careful to distinguish proposed improvements to the text from genuine Greek textual variants. Sometimes the text itself is uncertain and commentators have attempted to make suggestions as to the history or original form of the passage. But in these cases there are no Greek manuscripts which support the suggestion. Scholars are fond of pointing out, for instance, that John 21 seems to be an artificial addition to the Gospel since the original ending appears in 20:30–31. This chapter may indeed be an "epilogue," but there is no textual evidence suggesting that the Gospel ever circulated without it. The same is sometimes suggested for John's initial poetic verses about the "Logos" of God (John 1:1–18). Without it, the Gospel would have begun much like Mark with the story of John the Baptist. On occasion the suggestions are theologically motivated. For instance, the commentaries of Rudolf Bultmann,[19] G. H. C. MacGregor,[20] and Robert H. Strachan[21] often suggest rearrangements for the chapters of John or the elimination of individual verses which do not "fit." Bultmann made famous the view

---

18 While the punctuation of these verses may seem insignificant, it is crucial to understanding John 7. Jesus, at the water ceremonies of Tabernacles, is announcing that he is the festival's fulfillment. He is the source of living water that Tabernacles promises. For a detailed study of these verses and their theological significance see George Dunbar Kilpatrick, "The Punctuation of John 7:37–38," in *Journal of Theological Studies* 11 (1960): 340–42; J. B. Cortez, "Yet Another Look at John 7:37–38," *Catholic Biblical Quarterly* 29 (1967): 75–86, and Burge, *Anointed Community*, 88–93.

19. See Rudolf Bultmann, *The Gospel of John: A Commentary*, trans. G. R. Beasley-Murray, ed. R. W. N. Hoare and J. K. Riches (Philadelphia: Westminster, 1971).

20. G. H. C. MacGregor, *The Gospel of John* (Garden City, N.Y.: Doubleday, Doran, 1929).

21. *The Fourth Gospel* (London: SCM, 1941).

that an editor imposed on the gospel a "sacramental" emphasis, so Bultmann excluded words and verses that fit his hypothesis (see his remarks on John 3:5 and 6:52–59).

Bibliography

There are excellent books which can open up the subject of textual criticism for the beginner. Among these are:

Comfort, Philip W. *Early Manuscripts and Modern Translations of the New Testament.* Wheaton, Ill.: Tyndale, 1990.[22]

Finegan, Jack. *Encountering New Testament Manuscripts: A Working Introduction to Textual Criticism.* Grand Rapids: Eerdmans, 1974.

Greenlee, J. Harold. *Introduction to New Testament Textual Criticism.* Grand Rapids: Eerdmans, 1964.

———. *Scribes, Scrolls, and Scripture: A Layman's Guide to Textual Criticism.* Grand Rapids: Eerdmans, 1985.

Metzger, Bruce M. *The Text of the New Testament: Its Transmission, Corruption and Restoration.* Oxford: Clarendon, 1968.

Sitterly, Charles F., and J. Harold Greenlee. "Text and MSS of the NT" in Geoffrey W. Bromiley, ed. *The International Standard Bible Encyclopedia*, rev. ed., 4 vols. Grand Rapids: Eerdmans, 1979–1988: 4:814–22.

A much more technical study is Kurt Aland and Barbara Aland, *The Text of the New Testament.*[23] While this volume is not intended for the beginner, it is the most thorough study available in English and contains a complete list of available manuscripts, their abbreviations, what they contain, and where they are located (both in museums and in print). This volume also offers a superb chapter on the merits of the UBS³ and the NA²⁶ as well as instructions on how to use each Greek text and its critical apparatus (see pp. 218–62). A final chapter provides a guide to resources for working with the Greek New Testament (pp. 263–74).

---

22. Comfort's volume has the added value of being both clear *and* technically thorough. Pages 31–73 provide a complete list of manuscripts that will appear in any text apparatus.

23. Other technical studies include Frederick G. Kenyon, *The Text of the Greek Bible*, rev. by A. W. Adams (London: Duckworth, 1975), Ernest C. Colwell, *Studies in Methodology in Textual Criticism of the New Testament* (Grand Rapids: Eerdmans, 1969), and Bruce M. Metzger, *Chapters in the History of New Testament Textual Criticism* (Grand Rapids: Eerdmans, 1963).

The Greek text of the Fourth Gospel itself is surveyed in most of the technical commentaries. In particular, Schnackenburg[24] and Brown[25] have useful, brief discussions. In addition, a technical monograph study is available in Victor Salmon, *The Fourth Gospel: A History of the Text*,[26] and Philip W. Comfort has published "The Greek Text of the Gospel of John according to Early Papyri."[27]

24. Schnackenburg, *Gospel According to St. John*, 1:173–91.
25. Brown, *Gospel and Epistles*, 1:cxxix–cxxxvii.
26. Collegeville, Minn.: Liturgical, 1976.
27. *New Testament Studies* 36 (1990): 625–29. See the complete bibliography compiled by Gilbert Van Belle, *Johannine Bibliography 1966–1985: A Cumulative Bibliography on the Fourth Gospel* (Brussels, Belgium: Leuven University Press, 1988), 36–52.

5

The Literary Context

Following the guidelines in chapter 4 establishes the text. Now the exegete can feel confident that what he or she reads is as accurate as is possible. Next we must study the text as a literary unit—a story or set of paragraphs with an internal coherence and a relationship to other, similar paragraphs. Generally these other paragraphs shed light on the passage we are studying. Parallel or related accounts in the Synoptics or the Fourth Gospel need to be taken into account.

Synoptic Parallels

Only about 8 percent of John's verses directly parallel one of the Synoptic Gospels. Therefore, it is important to consider whether the passage we are exegeting is echoed elsewhere. As we witnessed earlier, many scholars are convinced that the Fourth Gospel drew heavily from the ancient historical sources which fed the Synoptics. A comparative study will unveil what changes John (or a Synoptic writer) might have made, or it might disclose an insight into the meaning of an episode in Jesus' life.[1]

In John 2:13–22 we read that on an early visit to Jerusalem, Jesus

---

1. Three helpful studies from the evangelical tradition can open this subject of the literary relation of John and the Synoptics: Archibald M. Hunter, *According to John: The New Look at the Fourth Gospel* (Philadelphia: Westminster, 1968), 36–48; Leon Morris, *Studies in the Fourth Gospel* (Grand Rapids: Eerdmans, 1969), 15–63, and Stephen S. Smalley, *John: Evangelist and Interpreter* (Greenwood, S.C.: Attic, 1978), 9–40.

"cleansed the Temple," driving out the animals and money-changers. This account is paralleled in all three Synoptics—with one significant exception. *In Matthew, Mark and Luke, the story takes place at the close of Jesus' ministry and forms a part of the reason for his arrest. John places the story at the beginning of Jesus' public ministry.* Did Jesus cleanse the Temple twice? Is only one account chronologically correct? Exegesis must take account of the particulars of historical detail, beginning with a careful comparison of the Synoptic and Johannine narratives themselves.

Or consider John 4:46–54, the story of the healing of the nobleman's son. Luke records something similar (7:1–10) as the healing of a centurion's servant. Both events take place in Galilee, but parallels seem few. Similar comparative studies can be made of the miraculous feeding of the five thousand (John 6:1–14; compare with Matt. 14:13–21, Mark 6:30–44, Luke 9:10–17). In this case John fills in the picture, completely showing the political enthusiasm of the crowd (John 6:15) and the teaching of Jesus about "bread from heaven" (6:35–71).

In some cases, a difficult decision must be made about the nature of the parallel. The miraculous catch of fish (John 21:1–14) well illustrates such a problem. Luke records a similar miracle (5:1–11) but sets it during the earthly ministry of Jesus. John's account is with the resurrected Christ. The many parallels lead us to ask: Do we possess two accounts of the same event (one in John the other in Luke) or did Jesus repeat this miracle on purpose to remind his followers of his power and authority in their lives?

Sometimes parallel texts exist outside the New Testament. Some of the apocryphal stories about Jesus that circulated in the early centuries of the church may contain historical reminiscences. For example, *The Acts of Pilate* reflects surprising similarities with John's passion account (John 18–19). Many sayings in *The Gospel of Thomas* echo the words of Jesus in John. Such parallels should be examined.

Considering parallels becomes easy with the right book. Unfortunately, not all gospel parallels include John. A popular volume, *Gospel Parallels*, B. H. Throckmorton, ed. (New York: Nelson, 1967), shows synoptic parallels in English but fails to include any Johannine material, even when it is significant. The following tools are best for work in Johannine parallels:

H. F. D. Sparks, ed. *The Johannine Synopsis of the Gospels*. New York: Harper, 1974. This older volume, based on the KJV, may appear difficult to use, but it lists countless parallels, even to phrases, in the Synoptics.

Kurt Aland, ed. *Synopsis of the Four Gospels*. Stuttgart, Germany: UBS, 1975. This edition, certainly the best, provides the Greek text on the left-hand page and English on the right. All parallels are given, though not in the sequence of the Fourth Gospel, so locating a passage can be troublesome. At the back (p. 341 and following) an outline of the parallels follows a reconstruction of Jesus' ministry. Indexes of all New Testament passages help. Use the index for John (pp. 360–61) to locate the text under study.

Robert W. Funk, ed. *New Gospel Parallels*, 2 vols. Philadelphia: Fortress, 1985. Extremely easy to use, the reference uses the English text and provides parallels outside the New Testament as well. Each Gospel has its own section, which first summarizes the parallels, then gives the complete texts. The unique feature in this effort is the wealth of information from such extra-biblical sources as the New Testament apocrypha and Nag Hammadi Papyri.[2]

The Macro-Context

Macro-Context describes the second step in a literary comparison of the Johannine passage. We must place the passage within the larger literary structure of the Gospel itself. Too often passages are studied in isolation, without regard for the literary context in which they were written. This context often gives the appropriate nuance to the meaning of individual verses under study.[3]

Chapter 3 explained the careful literary structure of the Fourth Gospel. A text being studied may be placed within the *Book of Signs* (chaps. 1–12) or the *Book of Glory* (13–21). Either of these "half-

---

2. Further apocryphal parallels can be culled from texts which study this literature directly. For example, Bentley Layton, *The Gnostic Scriptures: A New Translation with Annotations* (New York: Doubleday, 1987), provides a scripture index at the back in which Johannine parallels can be found. A similar index is available in Wilhelm Schneemelcher, ed., *The New Testament Apocrypha*, 2 vols., trans. A. J. Higgins, et al.; ed. R. M. Wilson (Philadelphia: Westminster, 1963–1966). The two-volume work edited by James H. Charlesworth, *The Old Testament Pseudepigrapha* (New York: Doubleday, 1983, 1985), while not offering a scripture index, does provide a lengthy topical index at the end of vol. 2.

3. A common example in Paul is 1 Corinthians 13. This passage is frequently used for everything from weddings to exhortations about love, yet many times the original intention of the text—a critique of charismatic enthusiasm that lacks love—is overlooked.

books" within the Gospel serves a specific purpose. Jesus' words within the Book of Signs present a public setting, often one filled with conflict. Or a text may intimately express Jesus' private teachings to his followers (as in chaps. 13–16). Either way, the larger context must be kept in mind. Once we note this larger setting, we can consider *where* in the Book of Signs or the Book of Glory this passage occurs. These two units have deliberate literary structures.

If we were studying Jesus' discourse on "the good shepherd" and the dispute that follows (John 10:1–39), we would first note that chapter 10 is part of Jesus' public ministry in the Book of Signs, in which John compares Jesus to the primary institutions of Judaism. We would need to decide if chapters 5–10 in the Book of Signs critique the Jewish festival system (Sabbath, Passover, Tabernacles, Dedication); if so, then Jesus' remarks in John 10 would have to be weighed in light of the circumstances of the Festival of Dedication mentioned in 10:22. But this introduces a difficulty. In the previous festival units, the festival is named at the beginning of the section (5:1; 6:4; 7:2), making it clear that the following section pertains to the feast. John 10 is different. The festival is named in 10:22, a fact that leads some scholars to wonder if 10:1–21 does not relate instead to the festival associated with chapter 9![4]

When we make this literary connection, valuable observations are at hand. If all of chapter 10 is linked to the Feast of Dedication, a study of the festival shows that Dedication recalled the historical period of the Maccabees, the corruption of the temple priesthood, and the need for faithful "shepherds" to guide the flock of God. Ezekiel 34 may even have been an Old Testament text commonly read in the synagogues during this time. Jesus simply exploits this setting, showing himself to be the shepherd to whom the Feast of Dedication looked.[5] Further, the final paragraph, 10:40–42, is evidently the closing of a major section in the Gospel. It concludes the festival discussion, sums up Jesus' work with signs, and sets the stage for the chapter 11 and the story of Lazarus.

---

4. Notice how 10:21 refers to the opening of the eyes of the blind as if this had just happened. In fact it has. This is the miracle of John 9. Therefore, some suspect, 10:1–21 is linked with what comes before, not with what comes after, namely, the Feast of Dedication.

5. Any exegesis of the notoriously difficult John 10:31–39 (esp. vv. 34–36) is helped greatly by a careful reference to the theological meaning of the Feast of Dedication. See the commentary notes of C. K. Barrett, *The Gospel According to St. John: An Introduction with Commentary and Notes on the Gospel Text*, 2d ed. (Philadelphia: Westminster, 1978), 385, and Raymond E. Brown, *The Gospel According to John*, 2 vols., in Anchor Bible Commentaries (New York: Doubleday, 1966–1970), 1:408–12.

Such literary comparisons face one problem: *How can we be certain about the structure of the gospel itself?* To be sure, scholars hold different views, but some tools help. First, most commentaries have introductory pages that discuss such themes as authorship, setting, and date. One section usually covers the Gospel's *literary form* but it may appear under a variety of names. Some commentators list literary form under *structure,*[6] *literary characteristics,*[7] *outline,*[8] *synopsis,*[9] *analysis,*[10] and *literary criticism.*[11] Brown's discussion is unmatched for its clarity, brevity, and common sense and is an excellent place to start for the beginning student.

Second, specialized studies have been published which analyze this literary structure and the larger unifying themes of the Fourth Gospel. While most of these studies attempt to follow individual themes in the Gospel, R. A. Culpepper, *The Anatomy of the Fourth Gospel: A Study in Literary Design*[12] has analyzed John as a literary phenomenon. This interdisciplinary study is by no means easy for the novice to read, but it fully repays careful study. As an example of narrative criticism, Culpepper analyzes the story, its characters, and its implied reader (the experience the story assumes the reader will have) and shows how they function together.

Other studies attempt to survey the narrative of the gospel and organize its major units. Among many such titles, the following are helpful:

Dodd, C. H. *The Interpretation of the Fourth Gospel.* Cambridge, England: Cambridge University Press, 1953. See pp. 289–443, especially 289–91.

Ellis, Peter F. *The Genius of John: A Composition-Critical Commentary on the Fourth Gospel.* Collegeville, Minn.: Liturgical, 1984.

Harvey, Anthony E. *Jesus on Trial: A Study in the Fourth Gospel.* Atlanta: John Knox, 1976.

---

6. J. H. Bernard, *St. John: Critical and Exegetical Commentary,* ed. S. R. Driver and A. Plummer (London: T. and T. Clark, n.d.), 1:xxx–xxxiii; Joseph N. Sanders and B. A. Mastin, *The Gospel According to St. John* (Peabody, Mass.: Hendrickson, 1987), 1–6; George R. Beasley-Murray, *John* (Waco, Texas: Word, 1987), xc–xcii, and D. A. Carson, *The Gospel According to John* (Grand Rapids: Eerdmans, 1991), 103–8.
7. Barrett, *Gospel According to St. John,* 5–15.
8. Brown, *Gospel and Epistles,* 1:cxxxviii–cxliv.
9. Barnabas Lindars, *The Gospel of John* (London: Oliphants, 1972), 70–73.
10. Leon Morris, *Gospel of John* (Grand Rapids: Eerdmans, 1970), 65–69.
11. Rudolf Schnackenburg, *The Gospel According to St. John,* 3 vols., trans. K. Smith (New York: Seabury, 1979), 1:44–58.
12. Philadelphia: Fortress, 1983.

Hengel, Martin. "The Author, his Pupils, and the Unity of the Gospel."
    In M. Hengel. *The Johannine Question*. Philadelphia: SCM/Trinity,
    1989. 74–108.
Kysar, Robert. *John's Story of Jesus*. Philadelphia: Fortress, 1984.
Morris, Leon. "John's Theological Purpose." In L. Morris. *Jesus is the
    Christ: Studies in the Theology of John*. Grand Rapids: Eerdmans, 1989.
    1–19.
Olsson, Bingur. *The Structure and Meaning of the Fourth Gospel: A Text-
    Linguistic Analysis of John*. Philadelphia: Coronet, 1974.
Painter, John. *Reading John's Gospel Today*. Atlanta: John Knox, 1975.
    3–18.
Smalley, Steven S. *John: Evangelist and Interpreter*. Greenwood, S.C.:
    Attic, 1978. See pages 85–121.

The Micro-Context

The final step in this literary study is to look for the internal
structure within the text itself. Having established the relationship
of the text to the rest of the Gospel tradition and to the balance of
the Fourth Gospel, we now seek to understand how the passage
is built and how its paragraphs and sentences are knit together to
form a coherent whole.

This again may be illustrated in Jesus' appearance at the Dedication Festival in John 10. At first glance it seems the passage is
divided into two halves, 10:1–21 and 10:22–39. Each half concludes
with conflict (10:19–21 and 10:39), and the halves are bridged by
the explicit reference to the festival (10:22). In the first half we read
about Jesus' shepherd metaphor and the Lord's interpretation,
while in the second half Jesus explains his own identity, in relation
to Abraham and then in relation to God. John 10:40–42 appears to
be a concluding paragraph, summing up the entire festival section.

Most commentaries will provide an analysis of these sections
to better organize their interpretation. But the best method is for
each exegete to work through the text alone, outlining and identifying changes in themes. If we were to examine chapter 10 in this
way, an outline might look like this:

A. Jesus' shepherd parable, 1–21
    1. The parable, 1–5
    2. *Response*: no comprehension, 6

3. Jesus interprets the parable, 7–18
4. *Response*: division, 19–21

B. Jesus' identity and divinity, 22–39
1. Jesus and Abraham, 22–30
2. *Response*: hostility, 31
3. Jesus and God, 32–38
4. *Response*: hostility, 39

C. Closing frame: Jesus and John the Baptist, 40–42
Closing the festival section of the Book of Signs

This exercise discloses the dramatic structure of the story. In each half Jesus is revealing something about his identity, first through the festival metaphor and then abstractly, in terms of Abraham and the Father. Each half enjoys connecting steps which transport the narrative to another plateau. And after each revelation there is a response. At first the crowd cannot comprehend what he means. This leads to divisiveness and finally to hostility. But Jesus will not be captured (10:39b) because he himself has power to control what happens.

Summary

Studying the literary context enables us to see the passage as a whole, break down its constituent parts, and understand the organization of its thought. A thorough knowledge of the layout of the Gospel itself, as we did in chapter 3, already gave us clues as to how the passage relates to surrounding texts. At this stage we simply look at the text in isolation, discovering its specific parallels in other literature (especially in the Synoptics) and discerning the thrust of its message.

Some writers have developed elaborate techniques to organize the thought of a biblical writer.[13] These work well, and if interest permits, they should be pursued. At the very least the context and form of the passage should be outlined so that every feature of its argument is accounted for and its pattern of thought carefully studied.

---

13. See Thomas Schreiner, *Interpreting the Pauline Epistles* (Grand Rapids: Baker, 1990), 97–126.

6

Building a Bibliography

Once the original text of the passage is secured (step one) and the literary context is understood (step two), it is a time to develop a bibliography, a cumulative list of books and articles by those who have studied the passage. What have other scholars seen in the text? What major literary or textual problems might have been missed?

Bibliographies

Where do we go to find good resources? A good starting point is to consult bibliographical books—which serve as guides to other books. Carefully study the table of contents or index of each bibliography to locate the appropriate section. Some of the better bibliographies include:

Aune, David. *Jesus and the Synoptic Gospels*. Downers Grove, Ill.: Inter-Varsity, 1980.

Fitzmyer, Joseph A. *An Introductory Bibliography for the Study of Scripture*. Rome: Biblical Institute, 1981.

Harrington, Daniel J. *The New Testament, A Bibliography*. Wilmington, Del: Glazier, 1985.

Martin, Ralph P. *New Testament Books for Pastor and Teacher*. Philadelphia: Westminster, 1984.

Metzger, Bruce M. *Index to Periodical Literature on Christ and the Gospels*. Grand Rapids: Eerdmans, 1966.

Osborne, G. *An Annotated Bibliography on the Bible and the Church*. Deerfield, Ill.: Open Door, 1982.

Scholer, David M. *A Basic Bibliographic Guide for New Testament Exegesis.* Grand Rapids: Eerdmans, 1973.

For older works on the Fourth Gospel consult E. Malatesta's volume, *St. John's Gospel, 1920–1965.*[1] This bibliography has been updated through 1985 by Gilbert Van Belle in *Johannine Bibliography 1966–1985: A Cumulative Bibliography on the Fourth Gospel.*[2] A thorough Johannine bibliography has been provided by Günther Wagner, *An Exegetical Bibliography of the New Testament: John and 1, 2, 3 John.*[3] Also helpful is the survey of Johannine studies compiled by Robert Kysar in *The Fourth Evangelist and His Gospel.*[4] Although not a bibliography per se, Kysar's work offers an impressive review of current literature. Its scripture index provides a key to major discussions in the text.[5]

Bibliographic Indexes

Three journals index the most current books and articles in biblical studies and may be consulted at academic libraries. *Elenchus Bibliographicus Biblicus*[6] comprehensively surveys books and articles relating to the Old Testament, New Testament, intertestamental Judaism, and early patristic periods. It lists many foreign language studies, and catalogues Ph.D. dissertations, making it a resource of inestimable worth.

Every exegete must become familiar with *New Testament Abstracts.* This indexing journal began in 1956 and is issued three times a year. It lists journals and books that pertain to the New Testament. The last number issued each year provides an index, which is generally bound at the end of the annual volume. In 1973 a comprehensive index of volumes 1–15 was published, simplifying use of the volumes to that date. Best of all, *New Testament Abstracts* gives a brief summary of each study catalogued so stu-

---

1. Rome: Pontifical Biblical Institute, 1967.
2. Vol. 82 of the Leuven University Press series *Bibliotheca Ephemeridum Theologicarum Louvaniensium* (Brussels, Belgium: 1988). This volume is currently available in the United States through Eisenbrauns, P. O. box 275, Winona Lake, IN 46590, for $94.50.
3. Macon, Ga.: Mercer University Press, 1987.
4. Minneapolis: Augsburg, 1975.
5. Another thorough review of Johannine studies is Gerald S. Sloyan, *What are They Saying about John?* (New York: Paulist, 1991).
6. *Elenchus Bibliographicus Biblicus* was published with the periodical *Biblica* from 1920–1968. Since 1968 it has been published independently in Rome.

dents can determine at a glance if a title is what they need.[7] It is organized by topic; when looking for the Fourth Gospel, users turn to the "Gospels" section and look for the subcategory on John. Most libraries carry *Religion Index One: Periodicals*,[8] which is traditionally shelved with other indexes to periodicals. *Religion Index One* is easy to use—especially for beginners—and quite current. It is important, however, to understand the *Religion Index One* scheme of organization. For the Fourth Gospel, first look up "Bible," then find "New Testament," and under that heading, "John." A related volume is *Religion Index Two: Multi-Author Works* (1960–). This index serves a similar function for multi-author works, festschrifts,[9] and collected essays.

Commentaries and Monographs

Don't hesitate to sleuth through a few commentaries in search of bibliography. Extensive lists of works usually appear at the end of volumes or after each section of exegesis. George R. Beasley-Murray's commentary, *John*,[10] for instance, lists works at the beginning of the section he is about to translate and study. Raymond E. Brown's *The Gospel and Epistles of John*[11] lists works at the end of each section. Therefore, a little detective work may be necessary! In addition, look at the end of each specialized study (or monograph) for a scripture index. This reveals where the author has given extensive attention to a particular passage.[12]

Computer-Assisted Searches

There is no substitute for turning the pages of an excellent indexing volume, but some new computer resources can do much of the hunting. A reference librarian can point out what sorts of tools are available for computer-assisted bibliographic searches.

---

7. *New Testament Abstracts* eliminates the need to use the indexes of most individual journals. The abstracts journal comprehensively reviews hundreds of journals published in many languages.
8. Early editions of the journal are called *Index to Religious Periodical Literature*. The journal was revised and its name changed, but the sequence of volumes remains unbroken.
9. Festschrifts (from Ger., *Festschriften*) are volumes of essays collected to celebrate the career of a noteworthy scholar.
10. Waco, Tex.: Word, 1987.
11. Collegeville, Minn.: Liturgical, 1988.
12. Such indexes, however, will not appear at the end of a commentary, since in them the texts are generally studied in the sequence of the chapters of the biblical book itself.

Some "on-line" search services exist solely as collections of information for researchers. One common computer base now available in many libraries is DIALOG® Information Retrieval Service in Palo Alto, California. John Hughes, a specialist in the use of computers for Biblical studies,[13] compares using DIALOG with flying a jet fighter: "the system is fast, accurate, complex, and powerful. Using it correctly, a knowledgeable person can quickly score direct hits."[14] But we might add that pilots do occasionally crash! DIALOG permits a researcher to enter subject-specific requests and combine terms. Best of all, DIALOG now has available *Religion Index One*, which means access to the most current updates. Unfortunately, at this writing religion indexes for 1959–1975 are not yet machine readable, but data entry for those years is underway.

The patron usually must pay to refer to DIALOG and similar communications services. Use of the religion index on DIALOG costs 80 cents a minute ($48 an hour), plus 15 cents for every online record.

The library may have free or more inexpensive computer resources, especially databases stored on high-density disks which can be explored though the use of the library's personal computer. Prepared by the American Theological Library Association, Wilsonline Information System® indexes *Religion Index One* (1949–1959, 1975–), *Religion Index Two* (from 1960), *Research in Ministry* (from 1981), and *Book Reviews in Religion* (from 1975). One distinct advantage of Wilsonline is that there is no cost to the researcher.

The wise bibliography hunter begins by asking for assistance from library staff, since successful computer-based searches require some degree of familiarity with what is sometimes called the program's "environment." Without doubt the database services are the tool of the future for bibliographic searches. With a basic understanding, they are easy to use, exhaustive, and extremely accurate.

How to Do a Bibliographic Search

I have decided to work on the story of the "woman at the well" in John 4. In two hours at the library I come up with the follow-

<hr>

13. See John T. Hughes, *Bits, Bytes, and Biblical Studies: A Resource Guide for the Use of Computers in Biblical and Classical Studies* (Grand Rapids: Zondervan, 1987). This volume is indispensable for any exegete who wants to know what's going on in the integration of computers and biblical research.
14. Ibid, 448.

ing results. First, I use Wilsonline, electronically reviewing all of *Religion Index One* from 1976–1989. I learn that files for 1949–1975 are not available. Calling for entries under "Bible (NT)/John" produces 386 articles on Johannine literature and theology. These citations may be quickly skimmed. Refining my search to "John 2–4/Criticism" gathers 226 entries. When my quick skim of the list uncovers an article that seems to pertain to my topic, I print the citation.[15] I also look for such possible index entries as "John 4," "Samaria," "women/John," "Jacob's well," "living water," and similar subjects found in the passage; forty-three "hits" look good.

Next stop is the *Elenchus Bibliographicus Biblicus* on the bound journal shelves.[16] In each volume John appears *after* Luke and Acts. Topical studies in John are listed first; then exegetical studies are organized around John's chapters. For example, section "G1.6" always contains articles on John 3–5. Even though many of these are not in English, some, nevertheless, look useful and readable. Searching the years 1980–1989 locates sixty-four monographs and articles on John 4, twenty-two of which were written in English; this was during the 1980s alone!

From the unbound journal shelves I then find *New Testament Abstracts*. The previous year's issues comprise three slim paper volumes. I check those, plus the latest issue. Under "Gospels/John," many articles are summarized but only two are on John 4. These, however, are new to my growing list; better still, they come from Africa! A creative find!

I also reach for a couple of commentaries whose authors are well known for their bibliographic sections. My favorites include Beasley-Murray and Brown. No doubt what they recommend on John 4 is worth a look. Beasley-Murray provides thirteen entries—some from major books I did not find in my earlier search. Brown lists eight sources, but only one in English.

If I want to search for works published before 1976 (recall that my computer search began there), I could skim the *New Testament Abstracts Index* in the reference section, or look at earlier volumes of *Elenchus*. For contributions published from 1920–1965, one handy tool is Malatesta's *St. John's Gospel, 1920–1965*. Full references are given for forty-nine titles on John 4 alone, fifteen of which are in

---

15. I decided for this search to work only with English language sources.
16. Some libraries shelve all indexes together instead of integrating them with other journals.

English. Cross-reference is made to fifteen more topical studies listed elsewhere in the volume.[17] In addition I glance at Van Belle's massive bibliography, which covers 1966–1985, looking for supplements to my ever-growing list. In addition, Günther Wagner's volume offers fourteen pages of bibliography on John 4 alone!

So far my sources have given me a list of ninety-six studies on John 4 in English alone! Some of these certainly overlap, for example, among titles listed in multiple sources, but I have found many more than fifty relevant bibliographic entries. Some will be more useful than others. With a little more work, I can narrow the list to perhaps twenty-five titles that are right on target.

But how can I know if a certain article is worthwhile? How can I get hold of a brief summary of an article without ordering it and reading it? This is where *New Testament Abstracts* comes in. For example, an article listing might be:

> J. D. M. Derrett, "[John 4:28] The Samaritan Woman's Pitcher," *Downside Rev* 102(1984)252–261.[18]

To get more details about this 1984 publication, I reach for New Testament Abstracts 1985. Always look for an article under the following year. Locate the author's name at the back of the volume and write down the "entry numbers" next to it. These can be looked up elsewhere in the volume. In the case of my test article, the "entry number" is 998 and the abstract printed in the book reads:

> 998. [John 4:1–42] J. D. M. Derrett. "The Samaritan Woman's Pitcher," DownRev 102(349,1984)252–261
> The "five husbands" of the Samaritan woman (see John 4:18) were the five senses, known to both Jews and Greeks. The woman left her pitcher behind (see John 4:28) because Jesus "the source" required neither pitcher nor wheel. The appendix discusses a Buddhist development of John 4:1–42.—D. J. H.[19]

---

17. Note that Malatesta gives each entry a number, so cross-references can be found quickly. Thus there are 3120 entries in the book, and numbers 1511–60 catalogue the Fourth Gospel.

18. That is, the article is in the journal, *Downside Review* (Bath, England), vol. 102, published in 1984. The article itself is found on pages 252–61. To find a table that translates the abbreviations of theology journals, look at the first few pages of the each year's first volume of *New Testament Abstracts* (*NTAb*).

19. D. J. H. are the initials of the writer of the abstract, in this case, Daniel J. Harrington, the general editor of *NTAb*.

Obviously Derrett is doing some interesting speculating about the symbolism of the passage! It is a very different sort of essay, but it might be interesting to study.

Such a thorough search leads beyond the conventional articles and books listed in well-worn commentaries and familiar journals such as *New Testament Studies, Catholic Biblical Quarterly,* and *The Expository Times.* Some downright fascinating articles may be found—even a few from non-Western cultures. Listed below is a mere sampling of articles on John 4 that I found, simply to show what can turn up with a bit of time in the library. Articles like these make all of our writing and research richer.

Ariarajah, Wesley. "The Water of Life [. . . John 4:37; 2:1]." In *Ecumenical Review* 34 (1982): 271–79.
Bligh, John. "Jesus in Samaria." In *Heythrop Journal* 3 (1964): 329–46.
Bowman, John. "Early Samaritan Eschatology." In *Journal of Jewish Studies* 16 (1955): 63–72.
Brown, Raymond E. "Roles of Woman in the Fourth Gospel." In *Theological Studies* 36 (December 1975): 688–99.
Bull, Robert. "An Archeological Context for Understanding John 4." In *Biblical Archeologist* 38 (1975): 54–59.
_____. "Archeological Footnote to 'Our Father Worshipped on this Mountain,' John 4:20." In *New Testament Studies* 23 (1977): 460–62.
Chappuis, Jean Marc. "Jesus and the Samaritan Woman; The Variable Geometry of Communication." In *Ecumenical Review* 34 (1982): 8–34.
Daube, David. "Jesus and the Samaritan Woman: The Meaning of Sygchraomai." In *Journal of Biblical Literature* 69 (1950): 137 47.
Derrett, J. D. M. "The Samaritan Woman's Purity (John 4:4–42)." In *The Evangelical Quarterly* 60 (1988): 291–98.
Eslinger, Lyle. "The Wooing of the Woman at the Well. Jesus, the Reader, and Reader-response Criticism." In *Literature and Theology* 1 (1987): 1647–83.
Kopas, Jane. "Jesus and Women in John's Gospel." In *Theology Today* 41 (July 1984): 201–5.
Manus, C. Ukachukwu. "The Samaritan Woman (John 4:7ff): Reflections on Female Leadership and Nation Building in Modern Africa." In *African Christian Studies* (Nairobi) 4 (1988): 73–84.
Niguidula, Lydia N. "'The Untouchable Touched,' John 4:1–30, 39–42." In *Asia Journal of Theology* 1.1 (Tokyo, 1987): 221–24.
O'Day, Gail R. "Irony and the Johannine Theology of Revelation: An Investigation of John 4." Ph.D. diss., Emory University, 1983.
Okure, Teresa. "The Johannine Approach to Mission: A Contextual Study of John 4:1–42." Ph.D. diss., Fordham University, 1984.

Pazadan, Mary M. "Nicodemus and the Samaritan Woman: Contrasting
    Models of Discipleship." In *Biblical Theology Bulletin* 17 (1987): 145–48.
Pryor, John W. "John 4:44 and the *Patris* of Jesus." In *Catholic Biblical Quar-
    terly* 49 (1987): 254–63.
Purvis, J. "The Fourth Gospel and the Samaritans." In *Novum Testamen-
    tum* 17 (1975): 161–98.
Robinson, J. A. T. "The 'Others' of John 4:38: A Test of Exegetical Method."
    In *StEv* 1 (1959): 510–15 (also in his volume, *Twelve New Testament
    Studies*. Naperville, Ill.: A. R. Allenson, 1962. See pp. 61–66).
Wedel, Alton F. "John 4:5–26." In *Interpretation* 31 (1977): 406–12.

A bibliography grows. As I look at these sources, I will take
note of references in footnotes and bibliographies. This is especially true of a Ph.D. dissertation. On this list Teresa Okure and
Gail O'Day each wrote dissertations on John 4. Their Ph.D. work
led them to compile extensive bibliographies that most certainly
are printed at the end of each volume.

Few libraries will have on hand all of the journals or books
required for your research. Some will certainly have to be ordered
from another university or seminary. A librarian will get these
resources for you through interlibrary loan.[20] In Chicago, where I
have done much of my research, twelve seminaries and nine theological libraries have a cooperative arrangement. That means
delivery of virtually any volume within days. *Still, all of this likely
will take time.* I know one reference librarian who growls audibly
when a student asks, "Could you get for me by tomorrow morning
volume 61 of *The Journal of Semitic Studies* from Manchester, England? My paper is due in two days!"

---

20 Sometimes there is a cost for ordering a book or article. Generally there is not. Some
institutions also may not send you a dissertation in which case it will have to be purchased
from *University Microfilms* in Ann Arbor, Michigan. Costs are as follows: For American dissertations sent to you on film, $27; softcover, $32.50; hardcover, $39. Prices for British disserta-
tions are considerably higher: film, $74; softcover, $127.50; hardcover, $137.50.

7

The Cultural Context

The text and its literary relationships are in hand; a decent bibliography begins to grow! Work is far from over, however. Next we go to the story itself, which contains hard-to-understand cultural pictures (waterjars or weddings), idioms ("bread from heaven"), and settings (the pool of Bethesda). We cannot assume to read the story as if it were penned last year in our native culture. An ancient story inevitably incorporates ancient characteristics to interpret.

Examples of cultural form abound in virtually every chapter of John. In chapters 5–10 Jesus' appearance at various Jewish festivals demands that we as interpreters know what these festivals mean. *No interpretation of John 6 is satisfactory without a comprehensive understanding of Judaism's Passover celebration.* Similarly, in John 13 Jesus washes the disciple's feet. Was this a peculiar thing for him to do? What role did footwashing play in the culture of the day?

Answers to these and other context-related questions must be found through research. What sources can unlock the culture of the first century so we can grasp John's message?

Commentaries

Thorough commentaries answer many context questions. But even the best commentators may overlook important details. A case in point is the discussion of John 7:53–8:11, the account of the woman caught in adultery. Few books adequately investigate the legal implications of adultery, the responsibilities of the witnesses, and the obligations of the judges. These insights must be found in specialized books (monographs), journals, and dictionary articles that surface during the bibliographic search.

Biblical Dictionaries and Encyclopedias

Among the most underused tools in the library, dictionaries and encyclopedias contain a wealth of information, presented concisely. However, use only the best books, those developed by responsible teams of scholars through current scholarship. Turning to such a volume, look up the words or ideas in question: *adultery, footwashing, weddings/Judaism, Pool of Bethesda,* . . . At the end of the best articles, bibliographic entries generally list further studies.

This is a list of some of the most helpful volumes commonly available for research in Biblical studies:[1]

> Achtemeier, Paul J., gen. ed. *Harper's Bible Dictionary.* New York: Harper and Row, 1985.
>
> Bromiley, Geoffrey W., gen. ed. *The International Standard Bible Encyclopedia,* 4 vols. Grand Rapids: Eerdmans, 1979–1988.
>
> Buttrick, George A., gen. ed. *The Interpreter's Dictionary of the Bible: An Illustrated Encyclopedia,* 4 vols. Nashville: Abingdon, 1962; Keith Crim, gen. ed., *Supplementary Volume, The Interpreter's Dictionary of the Bible.* Nashville: Abingdon, 1976.
>
> Douglas, J. D., organizing ed. *New Bible Dictionary,* 2d, rev. ed., N. Hillyer, rev. ed. Grand Rapids: Eerdmans, 1962.
>
> Elwell, Walter A., gen. ed. *Baker Encyclopedia of the Bible,* 2 vols. Grand Rapids: Baker, 1988.
>
> Myers, Allen C., revising ed. *Eerdmans Bible Dictionary,* rev. ed., 1 vol. Grand Rapids: Eerdmans, 1987.

Evangelical scholars deem the *International Standard Bible Encyclopedia* (*ISBE*) best among these works. This goldmine of information offers comprehensive articles, full bibliographies, and first-rate scholarship. One note is in order, however; this encyclopedia revises a set written in 1915 and rewritten in 1929. The older, dated

---

1. One note of warning: Libraries often hold dictionary sets on their reference shelves that carry more value as antiques than as research resources! Use only current works!

set often still sits on library shelves. Students many times fall into the trap of mistaking the old *ISBE* for current volumes. *The Interpreter's Dictionary of the Bible* carries similar stature, though to my mind, is not as complete. It is now becoming dated, and students must always consult the *Supplemental Volume*, which was added as a fifth book to the set in 1976.[2]

The Oxford Classical Dictionary is not a Bible dictionary at all, but the premier reference work for students who wish to know more about life in the Hellenistic world. This enriches Johannine research, particularly since some interpreters believe John's Gospel originated in Hellenism and borrowed extensively from its terminology, concepts and worldview. For example, *The Oxford Classical Dictionary* offers much on the Greek God Dionysus and related cultic festivals and explains the Hellenistic concept of *logos* (word) used in John 1. There are separate articles on Greek, Italic, Minoan, Persian, Roman, and Thracian religions, as well as on such topics as "sacrifice."[3]

Specialized Studies

Books that study the culture of first-century Palestine provide a window into everyday life. Sociology and anthropology are increasingly heard in—and contribute to—Biblical studies. In some cases, older books pertaining to sociological and anthropological issues remain exceedingly worthwhile sources. Volumes even from the nineteenth century may carefully examine the peasant cultures of Palestine, drawing accurate parallels to the biblical texts. With old studies good things are frequently buried where one least expects. The table of contents and indexes usually point the way to these hidden vistas. For instance, Alfred Edersheim's old volumes on the life of Christ contain one of the best descriptions yet of first-century Passover ritual culled responsibly from Jewish sources. *These sources have not changed!* And so, Edersheim's effort is still helpful.[4]

---

2. Recent printings of *The Interpreter's Dictionary of the Bible* employ a system to alert the reader to supplemental articles in volume five. If the original article contains an asterisk (*) at its heading, the *Supplemental Volume* contains more information.

3. N. G. L. Hammond and H. H. Scullard, eds., *The Oxford Classical Dictionary*, 2d ed. (Oxford, England: Clarendon, 1970).

4. Alfred Edersheim, *The Life and Times of Jesus the Messiah*, 2 vols. (repr. ed., Grand Rapids: Eerdmans, 1971). Some, however, have criticized Edersheim saying that he does not pay sufficiently close attention to the dates of his sources.

I keep these volumes within easy reach:[5]

Bouquet, Alan Coates. *Everyday Life in New Testament Times*. New York: Scribners, 1953.

Daniel-Rops, Henri. *Daily Life in the Time of Jesus*. Trans. P. O'Brian. New York: Hawthorne, 1962.

Daube, David. *The New Testament and Rabbinic Judaism*. London: University of London Press, 1956. Repr. ed., New York: Arno, 1973.

Derrett, J. Duncan. *Jesus' Audience: The Social and Psychological Environment in Which He Worked*. New York: Seabury, 1973.

_____. *Law in the New Testament*. London: Darton, Longman, and Todd, 1970.

Edersheim, Alfred. *The Life and Times of Jesus the Messiah*, 2 vols. Grand Rapids: Eerdmans, 1886. Repr. ed., Grand Rapids: Eerdmans, 1971.

Jeremias, Joachim. *Jerusalem in the Time of Jesus*, trans. C. Case. Philadelphia: Fortress, 1969.

Malina, Bruce J. *The New Testament World: Insights from Cultural Anthropology*. Atlanta: John Knox, 1981.

Matthews, Victor H. *Manners and Customs in the Bible*. Peabody, Mass.: Hendrickson, 1988.

Safrai, Schmuel, and M. Stern, eds. *The Jewish People in the First Century: Historical Geography, Political History, Social, Cultural, and Religious Life and Institutions*, 2 vols. Assen, the Netherlands: VanGarcum, 1976.

Schürer, Emil. *The History of the Jewish People in the Age of Jesus Christ*, 3 vols. Rev. ed., G. Vermes, et al., eds. Edinburgh: T. and T. Clark, 1973–1986.

Teringo, J. Robert. *The Land and People Jesus Knew: A Comprehensive Handbook on Life in First-Century Palestine*. Minneapolis: Bethany House, 1985.

Thompson, J. A. *Handbook of Life in Bible Times*. Downer's Grove, Ill.: InterVarsity, 1986.

A Sample Investigation

The story of the wedding at Cana (John 2) provides a good example. Jesus' first public miracle in John—the first of his signs—records a number of incidental cultural details. In fact, such contextual nuances vitalize the story. How amazing, then, that commentators and students run past these themes as if they were culturally familiar. The kinds of questions that should be asked include:

---

5. For additional sources see Gordon D. Fee, *New Testament Exegesis: A Handbook for Students and Pastors* (Philadelphia: Westminster, 1983), 93–100.

• Where is Cana of Galilee? Is it near Jesus' home village of Nazareth? Does its location mean anything? Did Cana have any messianic or political significance?

• How were weddings conducted in first-century Palestine? Who sent out the invitations? Who got invited?

• Is Jesus showing up unexpectedly? What were the obligations of guests? Why does Mary imply that Jesus ought to "do something" to correct the shortage of wine?

• Is Jesus rude when he says to his mother in verse 4, "Woman, what have you to do with me?"

• What are these water jars? Why does it say that they are stone? Is the volume they hold significant? Is the wine that is created absurd?

• The steward is conscious of the quality of the wine. What sort of wine was available? How was it made? When was it served? Did certain wine convey certain symbols in this culture?

• Since the story opens up the account of Jesus' messianic ministry, do marriages or abundant wine have anything to do with Judaism's messianic expectations?

As the study develops more observations—and more questions—will come to light. We may wonder who this steward is and what relations he has to the family and its guests. We need continually to raise our consciousness, however; culturally foreign elements exist in the text, and they need to be deciphered.

For purposes of this example we will limit the scope of our investigation to the subject of wedding customs. A quick look at the commentaries shows that this most basic detail is not generally emphasized. Where can we look?[6] The steps of our search might proceed as follows.

1. The 1988 revised edition of *The International Standard Bible Encyclopedia* (*ISBE*),[7] 3:261–66, includes a lengthy article

---

6. A partial answer to this question has been given in the bibliography of reference books listed above.

7. Geoffrey W. Bromiley, gen. ed., *The International Standard Bible Encyclopedia*, 4 vols. (Grand Rapids: Eerdmans, 1988).

and bibliography under "MARRIAGE; MARRY." Sections cover wedding rituals and even the symbolism of weddings in Judaism.

2. *ISBE*, 4:1024–26, s.v. "WATER," explains the use of water, waterpots, and ritual cleansing.

3. Bruce Malina's volume, *The New Testament World: Insights from Cultural Anthropology*[8] devotes a chapter to kinship and marriage. An unusual feature is that Malina compares first-century Jewish customs with American habits.

4. Victor Matthew's work, *Manners and Customs in the Bible*[9] is more difficult to use but, in another sense, more accurate. The cultural features of Judaism are divided by historical period, so I look under "Intertestamental and New Testament Period/Social Life."

5. Henri Daniel-Rops was a prolific Roman Catholic scholar who died in 1965. His *Daily Life in the Time of Jesus*[10] is unmatched for its clarity and organization. Pages 121–25 explain weddings using ancient Jewish sources.

6. J. Duncan Derrett's book, *Jesus' Audience: The Social and Psychological Environment in Which He Worked*[11] is one of the most useful on my shelf. An orientalist at the University of London, Derrett knows the world of the Middle East thoroughly and always seems to find a way of saying something new about the New Testament. The first chapter in his book, "The Social Scene," studies gender and parental authority, then goes on to discuss marriage customs.

7. Then I found pure gold in Derrett's *Law in the New Testament*.[12] He devotes a chapter to the cultural peculiarities of John 2:1–11, commenting on the wedding guests' reciprocity, Cana, Jesus' comment to Mary, and the miracle of the wine.[13]

8. Atlanta: John Knox, 1981. See pages 94–121.
9. Peabody, Mass.: Hendrickson, 1988.
10. Trans. P. O'Brian (New York: Hawthorne, 1962).
11. New York: Seabury, 1973.
12. New York: Humanities, 1970. See pages 228–46.
13. Derrett's footnotes are also a mine of information. Journal articles and even a full-length book on the Cana story—Ethel Stapana Drower, *Water into Wine: A Study of Ritual Idiom in the Middle East* (Amer. ed., Mystic, Conn.: Verry, 1965)—are given. As with many others in *Law in the New Testament*, this chapter originated as a technical journal article that a good bibliographical search would have located.

8. A technical, scholarly approach to the subject is next uncovered in Safrai/Stern.[14] This contribution is unusual because it buttresses comments almost exclusively on sources in the *Talmud* and the *Mishnah*.[15] Under "Home and Family" in volume 2, the index pointed out that pages 575–760 provide detailed descriptions of the wedding party, the types of food served, and even the customary seating assignments!

We do not need to employ all of these volumes to study this one cultural question. However using a few of them will alert us to cultural detail that will make our work in John 2 more rewarding.

We cannot predict what sort of discoveries may come our way. My cultural thinking was stretched when I listened to a literary/cultural study of the story of the woman at the well (John 4). This paper, read by Fredrick Niedner from Valparaiso (Ind.) University before the Society of Biblical Literature, suggests that John 4 actually describes *a Middle Eastern betrothal scene*! Other scholars (I have since learned) follow similar reasoning.[16]

It is a fascinating line of enquiry. Niedner compares the scene in John 4 with "well stories" of Isaac, Jacob, Ruth, Moses, and others. Some aspects of these stories fit John 4 wonderfully:

1. Travel is to a foreign land.
2. A woman is met at a well.
3. Water is drawn by one.
4. The woman retreats to her family.
5. An invitation is made to come to meet her family or village.
6. The time of day is almost always mentioned.
7. The character and genealogy of the woman is noted.

---

14. A common label for Schmuel Safrai and M. Stern, *The Jewish People in the First Century: Historical Geography, Political History, Social, Cultural, and Religious Life and Institutions*, 2 vols. (Assen, the Netherlands: VanGarcum, 1976). Fortress-Augsburg, Minneapolis, Minn., holds North American publication rights.

15. Another source of Talmudic tradition is found in J. B. Lightfoot, *A Commentary on the New Testament from the Talmud and Hebraica: Matthew–1 Corinthians*, 4 vols (Oxford, England, 1859; repr. ed., Grand Rapids: Baker, 1979). While certainly dated and selective, Lightfoot's compendium is often helpful. It should not, however, be our only avenue into the world of Jewish literature.

16. See Robert Alter, *The Art of the Biblical Narrative* (New York: Basic, 1981). See esp. pages 47–62.

8. There is often a negotiation and choice made, along with gift-giving.

I am not saying that this scene is Jesus' wedding, as if he were Jacob, but the message of the story is like a melody that here is being played out on the piano of Middle Eastern culture.[17]

We twentieth-century readers benefit when we learn what images would come quickly to mind to the original audience of the Gospel. Is John implying that Jesus' arrival and Jewish weddings have a good deal in common? Are the Cana wedding and John 4 to be compared? As the beloved Ruth was a foreign Moabite woman, so this woman is a Samaritan. All of these are valid and exciting questions. Their pursuit will make our exegesis not only exciting but rewarding.

---

17. Jesus would be, in effect, her seventh (her perfect) husband! Note even the bride-groom/bride metaphor in John 3:29: "He who has the bride is the bridegroom. The friend of the bridegroom, who stands and hears him, rejoices greatly at the bridegroom's voice. For this reason my joy has been fulfilled." In the chapter preceding John 4, John the Baptist calls Jesus "the groom."

8

Word Studies in John
Part 1: Word Searches

In all of our efforts thus far our goal has remained the same: to come as close as we can to the original intended meaning of the Fourth Gospel. Certain obstacles stand in the way—such as the ancient character of the story's language, structure, and culture— but with diligent and careful historical work we can approach the Fourth Gospel with far more interpretative confidence than we might have deemed possible.

The basic unit of meaning in any literature is the *word*. Words relate to each other, creating grammar, syntax, and sentences. The form of this grammatical structure also conveys meaning. The mechanics of putting words into thoughts is the essence of communication, so for any interpreter understanding how the mechanics work is the essence of exegesis. In most cases the mastery of Greek and its syntax is essential.[1]

However, once we understand the grammar and syntax of a sentence, we still have not dealt with the troubling problem of how to draw meaning from the word. Words derive meaning from their

1. See Thomas Schreiner, *Interpreting the Pauline Epistles* (Grand Rapids: Baker, 1990), 77–96; Scot McKnight, *Interpreting the Synoptic Gospels* (Grand Rapids: Baker, 1988), 51–56. For a more technical treatment see Anthony C. Thiselton, "Semantics and New Testament Interpretation," in I. Howard Marshall, ed., *New Testament Interpretation: Essays on Principles and Methods* (Grand Rapids: Eerdmans, 1977), 75–104, and David A. Black and D. S. Dockery, eds., *New Testament Criticism and Interpretation* (Grand Rapids: Zondervan, 1991). The last title is a comprehensive collection of nineteen essays by evangelicals on everything from hermeneutics and New Testament criticism to preaching.

literary context and from the wider *cultural environment* of the writer's day. For example, look at the text that opens this chapter. Thus far, including the chapter title, I have used the term *word* seven times in this chapter. I am assuming that my readers are familiar with the range of meaning possible for this combination of letters and are able to discern the particular meaning for the use of *word* in each sentence. Of course I meant by *word* a "part of speech." But what if someone wrote this sentence:

> The *word* became flesh and made his dwelling among us, full of grace and truth. And we have seen his glory.

What does *word* mean here? The author seems to mean something different from a part of speech. But how can we confirm that hunch? Clearly, two tools are needed. First, we need to ask, "What is the original context of this sentence? Can I compare this usage with a wider range of literature or speech—with more example sentences and paragraphs? Has the author used the word elsewhere?" Second, we need to ask, "Is the author assuming some knowledge on the part of his original reader, some information known in his day but now foreign? Is there a wider *literary* or *cultural context* that would help define this term, something the author presupposes?"

Another example might help. During the United Nations military action against Iraq in 1991—or even from the moment Iraq invaded Kuwait in August 1990, virtually everyone in the United States knew the acrostic *SCUD*. Before Iraq started firing these missiles against cities in Saudi Arabia and Israel, few people outside of the military intelligence community had heard the word. After the war it quickly fell into disuse and likely will be forgotten. But after the Gulf War began, few remained uninformed by the news about what a SCUD is, how it might be used, and its potential for destruction. Soon the culture of the day took over, and the word became a regular feature of vocabulary. By the time Strobe Talbott, an essayist in *Time*, penned the following sentence, he could anticipate being universally understood by the magazine's subscribers:

> Certainly by scudding Israel and launching oil slicks at desalination plants, Saddam justified expanding the war aims beyond the liberation of Kuwait.[2]

---

2. *Time*, Feb. 25, 1991, 24.

This sentence makes no sense whatsoever if we don't know what *scudding* means in the historical context of 1990–1991.[3] I overheard some students remark following an inspiring basketball victory, "Man, we scudded those guys!" *Scudded*? How will anyone in the future be able to interpret a sentence *like that*?

The basic element of meaning, the word, must be interpreted through its larger literary context as seen through the culture in which the word is used. This poses significant challenges when dealing with ancient texts. In Johannine studies we need to be able to survey the word-usage of John as well as to recognize the broader literary world in which he lived. Too often exegetes conclude that their task is complete when a text is studied "word by word," breaking the unit of communication down into smaller and smaller parts. But language does not work that way. Words are connected to literary-linguistic settings and it is these settings that convey thought.

So where do we begin? We need a strategy for understanding how John uses his terms. We need basic word-attack skills. And we need some help breaking into the cultural surroundings behind his Gospel so we may understand the larger linguistic environment in which the word lives.[4]

Fundamental Rules of Word Study

Darrell Bock has helpfully outlined three critical rules that must be followed whenever we think about words and exegesis.[5] Their simplicity is deceptive, however, because each rule levies a seri-

---

3. Following Iraq's conquest of Kuwait on August 2, 1990, an allied force led by the United States launched a military offensive against Iraq on January 15, 1991. A SCUD is a Soviet built short-range missile with conventional warheads which Iraq fired regularly at Israel and Saudi Arabia from mobile and stationary launchers.

4. One important interpretative issue not discussed in this chapter is whether an interpreter can ever recover the intended meaning of a text—modern or ancient. Some believe all interpretation is situational: The text does not have an absolute meaning in and of itself; all interpretations are simply the culturally conditioned response of the reader. See Anthony C. Thiselton, "The New Hermeneutic," in Marshall, *New Testament Interpretation*, 308–33; idem, *The Two Horizons: New Testament Hermeneutics and Philosophical Description with Special Reference to Heidegger, Bultmann, Gadamer, and Wittgenstein* (Grand Rapids: Eerdmans, 1984). See also the interesting popular discussion by Dinesh D'Souza, "Illiberal Education," *The Atlantic* 267.3 (March 1991): 51–79; see esp. 73–74. This subject will be discussed in chapter 10.

5. Darrell Bock, "New Testament Word Analysis," in Scot McKnight, ed., *Introducing New Testament Interpretation* (Grand Rapids: Baker, 1989), 97–113, esp. 98–99.

ous challenge on the exegete. By neglecting even one of them, most word study is in peril. These rules are:

1. Exegesis strives to uncover the meaning of words based on the meaning intended by the author for his or her original audience.
2. In order to uncover the precise meaning of a word, we must take care to study the word's full range of meaning.
3. Words derive their meaning from the context in which they are written.

First, exegesis strives to uncover the meaning of words based on the meaning intended by the author for his/her original audience. We are obligated, therefore, not to begin with our own sense or experience or emotional response, but instead look to the intention of the one who originally chose the word. In order for communication to be possible, authors must have ideas that can be shared with others—ideas that in some way correspond to ideas in the reader's mind. It is the task of the exegete to step into this circle of communication between original author and original reader to discover what is being said.

Second, in order to uncover the precise meaning of a word, we must take care to study the word's full range of meaning. Often we assume that with a quick glance at a lexicon or dictionary, we can learn the meaning of a word. But words change meaning. They have special nuances. Without some sensitivity to their connotation (or how they are popularly understood) we can misrepresent their meaning.

Third, words derive their meaning from the context in which they are written. This has already been illustrated regarding the terms *word* and *SCUD*. Bock remarks, "This point is crucial. Words as separate, isolated entities do not provide the key to the meaning of Scripture."[6] All words function in some relationship to other words, and therefore their context cannot be neglected.

Grammatical Analysis: Examining Original Sentences

For students who do not know Greek, grammatical analysis is especially troublesome. The original meaning John tried to convey

---

6. Ibid., 99.

is hidden in the Greek text, and those who do not have the ability to read John in Greek are at a severe disadvantage.

In chapter 4 we discussed the importance of studying the history, reliability and authenticity of the Greek text of the passage under study. Now a different assignment awaits us. We must learn what the original language—the original words and phrases—mean as we read them in the Gospel. Students who can work in Greek should strive to develop an agility and fluidity with the text, so that its nuances can be seen without undue reliance on such grammatical aids as an analytical concordance. Students from seminaries which emphasize the biblical languages will at once know a technique for breaking down the the structure of Greek sentences. Nouns, verbs, participles, adjectives and all parts of speech need to be accounted for.

For many, *diagraming* sentences is an excellent way to analyze the passage. Diagraming is not that dreaded assignment left behind somewhere in elementary school. On the contrary, it permits us to see exactly how an author's grammar works and how his argument hangs together. In one hermeneutics class at Fuller Theological Seminary, Daniel Fuller made each of us diagram the entire book of Philippians. I have kept the notebook to this day because it reminds me how serious labor can assist us in mastering God's Word.

There is no need to repeat the technique of diagraming here. Thomas Schreiner's helpful book, *Interpreting the Pauline Epistles*, provides a concise and helpful introduction.[7] Another, perhaps more simple, approach to structural analysis is given by Gordon D. Fee in *New Testament Exegesis: A Handbook for Students and Pastors*.[8] But for now we must simply affirm that, without a deliberate attempt to analyze the basic elements of the Greek text, exegesis will be handicapped.

Word-searches with Greek Concordances

How do I locate the places where John uses a certain word? How do I survey the literary context of the Johannine collection?

---

7. Grand Rapids: Baker 1990, 77–96; see also Scot McKnight, "New Testament Greek Grammatical Analysis," in McKnight, *Introducing*, 75–95.
8. Philadelphia: Westminster, 1983, 60–77.

Still working on the narrative of the woman at the well in John 4, I wonder about the use of the term *water* (ὕδωρ) throughout the chapter. After Jesus asks the woman for a drink of water, the following dialogue takes place:

> The Samaritan woman said to him, "How is it that you, a Jew, ask a drink of me, a woman of Samaria?" (Jews do not share things in common with Samaritans.) Jesus answered her, "If you knew the gift of God, and who it is that is saying to you, 'Give me a drink,' you would have asked him, and he would have given you living water." The woman said to him, "Sir, you have no bucket, and the well is deep. Where do you get that living water?" [John 4:9–11, NRSV]

The same text in Greek looks like this:

> λέγει οὖν αὐτῷ ἡ γυνὴ ἡ Σαμαρῖτις, Πῶς σὺ Ἰουδαῖος ὢν παρ᾽ ἐμοῦ πεῖν αἰτεῖς γυναικὸς Σαμαρίτιδος οὔσης; (οὐ γὰρ συγχρῶν-ται Ἰουδαῖοι Σαμαρίταις.) 10 ἀπεκρίθη Ἰησοῦς καὶ εἶπεν αὐτῇ, Εἰ ᾔδεις τὴν δωρεὰν τοῦ θεοῦ καὶ τίς ἐστιν ὁ λέγων σοι, Δός μοι πεῖν, σὺ ἂν ᾔτησας αὐτὸν καὶ ἔδωκεν ἄν σοι ὕδωρ ζῶν. 11 λέγει αὐτῷ [ἡ γυνή], Κύριε, οὔτε ἄντλημα ἔχεις καὶ τὸ φρέαρ ἐστὶν βαθύ πόθεν οὖν ἔχεις τὸ ὕδωρ τὸ ζῶν; [UBS³/Nestle-Aland²⁶ ed.]

Anyone who has worked in John knows how the author enjoys using double meanings. Here is an example. Is something more being represented by the word *water* in John's theology? Is this passage only about the way Jesus quenches his thirst on the road north, or is more implied?

To answer such questions I first must ask some procedural questions: How can I locate every reference to water (ὕδωρ) in the Fourth Gospel? Once I find these references, how do I accurately determine the word's context? What tools are the best for this? It is essential to keep in mind that all word searches must be driven by the Greek text of the New Testament. Sometimes the English text may use the word *water* in places where ὕδωρ does not appear in the Greek.

In order to develop a word-count of ὕδωρ in John, I can turn to Robert Morgenthaler's *Statistik des Neutestamentlichen Wortschatzes.*[9]

---

9. Zürich: Gotthelf, 1958.

This book is in German, but it is a useful index of Greek words and gives their frequency of occurrence in the New Testament. At once I learn that ὕδωρ occurs in Matthew seven times, Mark five times, Luke six times, John twenty-one times, Acts seven times, Paul one time (Ephesians), Hebrews two times, James one time, 1 Peter one time, 2 Peter three times, the Johannine epistles, four times, and Revelation eighteen times.

So ὕδωρ appears a total of seventy-six times in the New Testament, twenty-one of which occur in John. I make special note of the four references in the epistles of John; I should particularly look for ties there.[10] It is clear that, in comparison with the other gospels, the Johannine usage is unusually high and no doubt specialized.[11] Morgenthaler gives me the information quickly and effortlessly.

I might also have used a Greek concordance that lists word frequencies and where they appear. The best, and the most current, volume is H. Bachmann and H. Slaby's book, *Computer Concordance to the New Testament*.[12] Although it is a technical German volume, it is accessible to the average student. The introduction, as well as all entries, are given both in English and German, and the number of occurrences is shown for each Greek word entry.[13]

Another popular volume is the Greek concordance edited by W. F. Moulton, A. S. Geden, and H. K. Moulton, *Concordance to the Greek New Testament*.[14] This volume not only gives me an accurate count of the uses of ὕδωρ; it also quotes the phrase in which the word occurs. Even though an older work than the Bachmann/Slaby volume, the fifth edition of "Moulton/Geden" reflects the complete text of the current UBS³/NA²⁶ Greek text. Using these Greek

---

10. Most scholars agree that the epistles of John share the same milieu or setting as the Gospel, although written at a different time. The Apocalypse is more difficult. While many are convinced that this too is a Johannine writing, others are less confident. At least we can say that it is a different form (or genre) of writing, and its use of language is considerably different. I have chosen to limit my work to the Fourth Gospel and (to a lesser extent) the Johannine epistles.

11. It is important to keep in mind that I am not just interested in the occurrences of the nominative form, ὕδωρ. I need to take into account all uses of this word in different forms (ὕδατος, ὕδατι, etc.). This becomes especially important in computer driven concordance searches. H. Bachmann and H. Slaby, *Computer Concordance to the New Testament* (New York: de Gruyter, 1980) takes all Greek forms into account.

12. See note 11.

13. In addition, the concordance places an asterisk [*] alongside each reference which represents a major textual variant. These disputed references must always be taken into account.

14. 5th ed., (Edinburgh: T. and T. Clark, 1978).

concordances we learn that twenty-four verses use the word, although three of these are variant readings: 3:8, 5:3, and 5:4.

Word Searches with Personal Computers

Text searches by computer are becoming an increasingly popular way to analyze words or concepts within the Greek, Hebrew, or English text. Each new generation of software brings more accuracy, speed, and flexibility. Newer programs allow the area of the Bible searched or the forms sought to be quite specific.[15] There are many programs on the market, most of which do an efficient job.

On an IBM® (or compatible) computer a number of products permit searches of the entire text of the Bible or simply the Greek New Testament. For students working in the English Bible, *Quick-Verse* (Parson's Technology, Cedar Rapids, Iowa) is inexpensive and easy to use. Another excellent choice is *WORDsearch* (WORDworks Software Architects, Austin, Tex.). *BibleSource* (Zondervan Electronic Publishers, Grand Rapids, Mich.) offers English texts, such as the New International Version, and adds the *NIV Study-Bible*[16] notes. Further modules for *BibleSource* allow such add-on tools as the *NIV Bible Dictionary*,[17] the *NIV Exhaustive Concordance*,[18] other translations, the Greek New Testament, and even the Hebrew Old Testament. This will enable the personal computer (PC) user to build a Bible research and reference center into the computer!

Even with computer-base searches, using the Greek text takes the student a step closer to superior results. For PC users this can be done through one of the popular English programs, such as *BibleSource*, where the Greek text can be added on. *NIVpc* (Zondervan) displays the NIV text and the Greek New Testament in parallel windows. Unfortunately this program at this writing does not use the standard UBS³/NA²⁶ Greek text.

15. One can, for example, reconstruct the concordance of Moulton/Geden by searching for all uses of ὕδωρ but in your own search you can require that a context range of, say, six or seven verses above and below the occurrence be given. This can then be printed.

16. Kenneth Barker and Donald Burdick, eds., *The NIV Study Bible* (Grand Rapids: Zondervan, 1985).

17. Merrill C. Tenney, gen. ed., *The New International Dictionary of the Bible*, J. D. Douglas, rev. ed. (Grand Rapids: Zondervan, 1987).

18. Edward W. Goodrick and John R. Kohlenberger, eds., *The NIV Exhaustive Concordance* (Grand Rapids: Zondervan, 1990).

One outstanding tool for Greek text searches is produced by The Gramcord Institute.[19] Here a student may search the Greek New Testament for specific grammatical forms of a word. This is a brilliant addition; after turning on programed grammatical and syntactical keys, the student can search for only one grammatical combination (such as: *search + pres. act. infinitive*). Another program will retrieve every lexical form of a word, regardless of gender, number, case, tense, or mood, giving searches a thoroughness previously unavailable. In addition, this software program is fully compatible with multilingual wordprocessors, including *ChiWriter*, *WordPerfect with Scripture Fonts*, and *Nota Bene*.[20]

Users of IBM or compatible computers with a graphics capability may be helped by Word Publishing Company's *WordSoft*, a lineup of programs offering search features in the Greek, Hebrew, and English texts (various translations), using dazzling graphics and color. It even offers such study aids as *Strong's Greek/Hebrew Dictionary*.[21] Hit two keys and a window opens on the screen, displaying the Greek or Hebrew root. Its *Advanced Study System 3.0* permits up to ten windows to be open. Like Gramcord's grammatical program, Advanced Study System 3.0 allows searches keyed to Greek lexical forms.

The Macintosh computer is ideal for Scripture searches because of the ease with which graphics can be added to text and the clear resolution of its display screen. It is also designed to be "user-friendly," meaning the system doesn't require a lot of knowledge of computers to be operated. Students tend to gravitate to the "Mac" when a choice of systems is available, and with only a short orientation time they achieve satisfying results. Linguist's Software of Edmonds, Washington offers an excellent program for the Greek New Testament.[22] Linguist's *Anytext Search Engine* is

---

19. The Gramcord Institute, 8435 N. E. Glisan St., Portland, OR 97220. Phone, (206) 576–3000, FAX (503) 761–0626. At this writing Gramcord's programs are only designed for IBM (and compatible) PC users; but Paul Miller, who heads Gramcord, promises that a Macintosh version is coming.

20. Greek and Hebrew fonts can also be added to such wordprocessors as *WordPerfect*. Zondervan Electronic Publishing offers *Scripture Fonts* for this purpose.

21. James Strong, *The Exhaustive Concordance of the Bible* (1890; rev. ed., Nashville: Abingdon, 1980). The dictionary is located at the back of the volume, after the concordance.

22. Linguist's Software, Box 580, Edmonds, WA 98020. Phone, (206) 775–1130. This company sells software programs for Greek and Hebrew text searches and can supply fonts in more than 200 languages.

designed to handle technical Greek searches and works with virtually any English translation. Another Macintosh program that is superior in its simplicity and ease of operation is *MacBible* (Zondervan). It permits searches of the entire Bible or only part, using a window of the computer screen. It is possible to see text on one "window" on the screen, while searching with English, Greek, or Hebrew *MacBible* in another window. This popular format is called the "windows" environment. Programs such as these should be assessed by (1) how easy they are to us; (2) the technical support that is available (such as a phone number to call for advice or troubleshooting), and (3) the ease with which the software can be installed and set up. *MacBible* scores high on all three. Its manual, which was written and designed by William Mounce, is a model of thoroughness and clarity.[23]

My computer search of ὕδωρ found twenty-one occurrences in John. This is the same number that I have seen in other sources and excludes variants. However, one caution is necessary regarding a computer word search. Most software programs will only search for the term you request; they do not recognize changes through, say, inflection or declensions. Better programs will not present this problem. A search which only locates instances of ὕδωρ is not good enough since ὕδατος, for example, would be omitted. I set up a search for words that included the characters ὕδ, which means I was looking for the stem of ὕδωρ. In the process, however, I also encountered other words which begin with ὕδ (for instance, ὑδρία, "waterjar," appears in John 2:6 and 4:28). And I probably want to be careful to exclude these words from the search. Also, if an irregular verb or noun is being searched, its stem may change. Therefore, word-searches can only be done when all forms have been found in a Greek lexicon.[24] Searches on Gramsearch (from Gramcord), do take into account these diverse lexical forms.

---

23. Like BibleSource, WordSoft, and Gramcord, MacBible plans to add several modules, including the Septuagint. Currently the Apocrypha and the Hebrew Old Testament are also available, as well as English texts in the KJV, RSV, NRSV, and NIV. Unfortunately, Zondervan, the maker of MacBible, has not designed the program for searches that are keyed to lexical forms or syntax (although this data is available). Hopefully this will be forthcoming in an upgrade. Without it, MacBible is seriously handicapped.

24. Looking up a word in Walter Bauer, et al., *A Greek-English Lexicon of the New Testament and Other Early Christian Literature*, 2d ed., trans. W. F. Arndt (Chicago: University of Chicago Press, 1979) gives all forms as they appear in the New Testament. If the word does not appear with great frequency, *BAGD* will provide all references in the text and virtually do the concordance search for you. On using *BAGD*, see chapter 9.

English Language Searches

For students who do not know Greek, a word search in the English text for further references is more difficult but not impossible. Sometimes words appear in the English translation to make the text more understandable which have nothing to do with the original. For example, the NIV for John 2:6 refers to "stone water jars" but the word *water* (ὕδωρ) is not in the Greek text. The first step is to make sure that the English translation used is as close to a word-for-word rendering of the original Greek as is possible. For example, the Revised Standard Version (or its 1991 revision, the New Revised Standard Version) provides an excellent text from which to work. A search based on the Living Bible paraphrase or even a "dynamic equivalent" translation such as the New International Version can present difficulties since the wording may not follow the Greek.

Another trick for following the use of Greek words in English when you want to be sensitive to the Greek but cannot read it well is to employ an interlinear Greek/English New Testament. This is a volume which prints the Greek text but adds an English translation underneath. Figure 6 illustrates what a line from a typical interlinear would look like for John 4:11.

λέγει	αὐτῷ	[ἡ γυνή],	Κύριε,	οὔτε	ἄτλημα	ἔχεις	καὶ
says	to him	(the woman)	sir	no	bucket	you have	and

το φρέαρ	ἐστὶν	βαθύ·	πόθεν	οὖν	ἕξεις	τὸ ὕδωρ	το ζῶν;
the well	is	deep	from where	then	do you have	the water	—living

Notice how easily each word aligns with its Greek equivalent. While many of these interlinears are available, in 1990 Tyndale Publishers printed an excellent edition of the *New Revised Standard Version* (used above) along with the most recent edition of the Greek New Testament (the UBS[3]/Nestle-Aland[26]).[25] Many others available as well.[26] It is even possible to find Greek texts which are

---

25. J. D. Douglas, ed., *The New Greek English Interlinear New Testament*, trans. R. K. Brown and P. W. Comfort (Wheaton: Tyndale, 1990).

26. For instance, Zondervan offers an entire list, including interlinears for the NIV and the NASB.

printed in parallel columns with the English so the two can be read side-by-side.[27]

In order to do a search, a *concordance* is needed. Concordances are indexes of words showing where they appear in the Bible. *Exhaustive concordances* give a list of all occurrences and so are better suited to a thorough search. Further, concordances are always based on one English translation. Hence, there is *The Exhaustive NIV Concordance* (Zondervan), *The Eerdmans Analytical Concordance to the RSV* (Eerdmans), *Young's Analytical Concordance to the KJV Bible* (Eerdmans), and *Strong's Exhaustive Concordance of the KJV Bible* (Abingdon). Libraries typically carry shelves of these but only the most current volumes should be used.

The best English concordances are *analytical*, that is, they analyze the English word based on the Greek word behind it. For instance, *Young's Analytical Concordance*, while based on the King James Version, requires that I look up "water" and then look for the secondary entry: "3. water, ὕδωρ, hūdōr." Here under "John" are all references to ὕδωρ[28]. The Revised Standard Version can be similarly searched using *The Eerdmans Analytical Concordance to the RSV*. In this case the entry is followed by a series of numbers [16], which are keys to Greek and Hebrew words. Under "John" all entries are given, followed by the key "14," which tells us that these uses of *water* actually are translations of ὕδωρ. From here I can make a list of entries and look up the contexts.[29]

Creating a Wordsearch Table

Next I need to organize the information about the word under study. The best way is to create a chart in which the references are listed (along with variant or disputed readings) and then once these

---

27. See *The Zondervan Parallel New Testament in Greek and English* (Grand Rapids: Zondervan, 1988). The United Bible Society publishes a critical edition of the Greek New Testament with the English RSV text on the opposite page. For everyday use, this volume is an outstanding investment.

28. Keep in mind, however, that Young's concordance is quite old (its publisher does not even include its original date) and cannot be a reliable guide to current Greek texts. The same limitations apply to a similar English concordance, Strong, *Exhaustive Concordance*.

29. Another concordance to the RSV is John W. Ellison, Nelson's *Complete Concordance of the Revised Standard Version of the Bible* (New York: Nelson, 1957). While it is exhaustive it does not refer to any original Biblical language texts. The same is true of Goodrick and Kohlenberger, *NIV Exhaustive Concordance*.

are looked up, the texts themselves can be studied and notes supplied. A typical word-search chart for ὕδωρ appears on the following two pages. Note how each entry has been given careful attention.

Take a moment to study the chart in figure 7, noting some of the significant observations that come to mind. It is clear that John uses ὕδωρ in commonplace ways, such as when he mentions the water at the pool in chapter 5. But it is clear that his interest is also symbolic. Note that there are important connections among the words *life*, *water*, and *spirit*. In fact, water seems either to be a symbol of the older Jewish institution—which is about to pass away or be supplanted by Christ (as the water of Cana or the pool at Bezatha)—or it seems to be a symbol of the newness that Christ brings, the gift he offers.

In chapter 1 water accompanies Jesus' inauguration and anointing in the Spirit. In chapter three, Nicodemus learns that rebirth must incorporate this "water and Spirit." In chapter four it is precisely this mysterious water that the woman is offered and finally requests. And in chapter 7 at the Tabernacles festival Jesus makes an announcement in the midst of the water ceremonies that *he has water to offer too!* Likely 7:37–39 are key verses that make an explicit connection: Living water is actually the Spirit which would come with Christ's glorification on the cross. Is it any surprise, then, that in 19:34, when Jesus is stabbed with a lance, water—this mysterious water—pours forth? Even 1 John affirms these themes of new life, Spirit, and water as major parts of John's Christology and ecclesiology.

A thorough study of John 4 and its discussion of "water" must take into account the literary context of the author's writings. It so happens that, for him, this is a unique and important term which carries a great deal of theological freight. But without some survey of his writings, this insight into the chapter would have been lost to me.

Thesaurus Linguae Graecae for the Advanced Student

Advanced students of the Greek New Testament realize that many words in the New Testament appear infrequently. Their meaning must be determined in a comparative search through extrabiblical texts. But how can we survey the occurrences of an important Greek word in nonbiblical literature?

Figure 7. Word Study Chart: ὕδωρ (Water) in the Johannine Literature

Text	Key Words	Context/Notes
1:26	ἐν ὕδατι	John the Baptist says that he baptizes in water. Is water a constant symbol of renewal or spiritual refreshment in Judaism? Does water represent a "new beginning" or "newness" in the Gospel?
1:31	ἐν ὕδατι	John the Baptist describes his mission of baptizing in water so that Jesus might be revealed to Israel.
1:33	ἐν ὕδατι/ἐν πνεύματι ἁγίῳ	John refers to the baptism of Jesus. The Holy Spirit arrives during Jesus' water baptism. Are water and Spirit linked in this Gospel?
2:7	ὑδρίας ὕδατος	Jesus commands servant at the Cana wedding, "Fill the jars with water!"
2:9	ὕδωρ	The water has "become wine." Note: water is connected to the new thing that God is doing in Jesus.
2:9	ὕδωρ οἶνον	The steward tastes the water now become wine.
3:5	ἐξ ὕδατος/πνεύματος	To Nicodemus (3:5–8), Jesus says we need to be born "of water and the Spirit" in order to enter the Kingdom of God. Water and Spirit are again linked.
[3:8]	ἐξ ὕδατος/πνεύματος	weak variant. The original likely referred to "those born of the Spirit," but a scribe expanded it making this verse parallel 3:5.
3:23	ὕδατα	Narrator's explanation about Salim, where John the Baptist worked "because there was much water there."
4:7	ὕδωρ	This (and 4:10–15) is the story of the woman at the well in Samaria. She comes to this well to draw water. Water is the content of this Jewish well.
4:10	ὕδωρ ζῶν	Jesus offers "living water" and refers to "the gift of God" he can supply!

4:11	ὕδωρ τὸ ζῶν	The woman inquires how Jesus can obtain "living water." What does "living water" mean for John?
4:13	ὕδατος	Jesus says that this water in this well will lead to further thirst.
4:14	ὕδατος	Jesus mentions his own water, which eliminates thirst forever.
4:14	ὕδωρ	Jesus offers different water.
4:14	ὕδωρ/εἰς ζωὴν αἰώνιον	Jesus' water creates a spring of water leading to eternal life.
4:15	ὕδωρ	The woman asks Jesus for this water so that she might drink.
4:46	ὕδωρ οἶνον	A reminder that Cana is where Jesus made water into wine.
[5:3]	ὕδατος	weak variant. The explanation of the miracle at the pool of Bethesda.
[5:4]	ὕδατος	weak variant. The explanation of the miracle at the pool of Bethesda.
5:7	ὕδωρ	The lame man wants Jesus to put him into the pool of water.
7:38	ὕδατος/ζῶντος/πνεῦμα	Jesus' offer of living water (Holy Spirit, v. 39) at Tabernacles.
13:5	ὕδωρ	Jesus pours water into the basin to wash the disciples' feet.
19:34	αἷμα/ὕδωρ/(πνεῦμα)	On the cross, Jesus is stabbed and blood and water pour from his side. Note that the Spirit is mentioned in verse 30 when he dies on the cross.

Uses of ὕδωρ in the Johannine Epistles

1 John 5:6	ὕδατος/αἵματος	Note connection between water and blood (twice). This text may be important. "This is he who came by water and blood, Jesus Christ, not with the water only but with the water and the blood." Does this link up with John 19:34?
1 John 5:6	ἐν τῷ ὕδατι καὶ ἐν τῷ αἵματι	See above.
1 John 5:8	πνεῦμα/ὕδωρ/αἷμα	Water and blood again linked. But now the Spirit is added as in the Gospel. Note 5:7–8: "And the Spirit is the witness, because the Spirit is the truth. There are three witnesses, the Spirit, the water, and the blood; and these three agree."

The University of California at Irvine launched a 15-year, $6 million project to create a databank of all Greek authors and their works from Homer (about 700 B.C.) to A.D. 600. In 1987 the *Thesaurus Linguae Graecae* (or *TLG*) was completed (except for corrections). It contains 60 million words, reflecting 2900 Greek authors and 8400 literary works. Imagine the resources this gives a scholar who may now survey the use of any Greek word in antiquity!

Originally, access to this database could be achieved only through the IBYCUS system, a computer dedicated strictly to the *TLG*. Costing many thousands of dollars, it was available only in libraries. Today the *TLG* is available on a CD ROM disk and may be accessed by software that can be placed in a PC hard drive.

IBM or compatible computer users may employ a software program called *LBase* (now in version 5.1) from Silver Mountain Software.[30] Macintosh users can purchase *PANDORA*, a complex retrieval Hypercard program, which, like *LBase*, conducts searches, displays the references in context, and exports them to a variety of formats such as Microsoft Word or WordPerfect.[31]

A useful way to navigate your way through the myriad of authors and texts in the *TLG* is available in an index volume, L. Berkowitz and K. A. Squitier, eds. *Canon of Greek Authors and their Works, Second Edition (for Thesaurus Linguae Graecae)* (Oxford: University Press, 1986).

Summary

This, then, is the first step in any exegetical examination of a word in the Fourth Gospel. But, as I said at the beginning of this chapter, this is only half the battle. The further question is whether John played on meanings commonplace in the world of his day. From the Johannine literary context we must move to *the wider linguistic world of the first century*. This will include the other writings of the New Testament, the Old Testament, and even extrabiblical literature as these relate to our work.

---

30. For *LBase*, contact Silver Mountain Software, 7246 Cloverglen Drive, Dallas, TX 75249, ph., (214) 709–6364.
31. For *PANDORA* contact The Perseus Project, Department of the Classics, 319 Boylston Hall, Harvard University, Cambridge, MA 02138, ph., (617) 495–9025.

9

Word Studies in John
Part 2: Word Meanings

When the Gospel of John employs words, does it refer to some larger, underlying framework, an important pool of metaphors now lost to us? Was there a literary setting to which the gospel was indebted? Let's return for a moment to chapter 8's study on water (ὕδωρ). It would be helpful to determine whether other literature in the Hellenistic Judaism of John's day gives us insight into the use of this word as a theological metaphor or whether other New Testament writings help us. And what about the Old Testament? Certainly the images and concepts found there informed any pious Jewish writer in the first century. Was water employed along with life and spirit in popular theological writing or speech?

Answering these questions is a difficult chore since we now include literature both outside and inside the New Testament— indeed we must journey outside the religious literature of the Bible altogether. Few are able to read and recall the enormous literature available. Fortunately, inclusive tools at hand broaden the scope of our study effortlessly and effectively. Scholars (and Ph.D students) have combed these writings for us; the benefits of their labors are available.

Moreover, these works do more than assess the significance of the words we study. They also discuss the Fourth Gospel and the entire New Testament, helping to integrate these insights into our exegesis of Scripture. They are not simply esoteric catalogues of antiquity but frequently provide the keys to unlock remarkable insights into the Gospel. Consider again the word *water*. Palestinian Judaism and the Old Testament viewed "abundant water" as a symbol of the coming Day of the Lord.[1] In a climate subject to frequent draughts it is no surprise that Israel would look to God's ultimate blessings with this idea in mind. Jewish writings even taught that an eternal spring would gush right out of Jerusalem and flow down the mountain! This abundance evolved into a symbol for the generous outpouring of the Holy Spirit that would come with the Messiah.

Such insights allow us to step behind the Fourth Gospel and comb the themes of Judaism and the ancient world.

First, do not neglect the longer reference encyclopedias and dictionaries (for example, *The International Standard Bible Encyclopedia*[2] and *The Interpreter's Dictionary of the Bible*[3]). Each of these reference works may offer some study of a word commonly used in the text of the Gospel. "Water," for instance, is an entry in nearly all of them. But technical terms crucial to John, such as *remain* or *abide* (μένω, *menō*) or even basic terms, such as *faith* (πιστεύω, *pisteuō*) will often be absent. So while these tools may be helpful, their usefulness has significant limitations.

Second, the full use of concordances can provide entry into the Old Testament and the balance of the New Testament. The prophetic use of *water* as an eschatological image could be located this way. But frequently there is such an abundance of references that some guide is need to abbreviate the search and point out those passages which are essential. Concordances to the writings of other literature in antiquity do exist, but a thorough knowledge of Greek is essential to efficiently use most of them.[4]

---

1. Even "living water" has a specialized use. It represents "running water," compared with "standing" water, as in a well or cistern. Since the former was precious, it was valued and began to take on symbolic features. The Dead Sea Community at Qumran, for example, worked to make sure that "running" or "living" water was available for their ritual baths. Visitors often marvel at Qumran's complex aqueduct system, which made these baths possible. Imagine the exegetical significance this has for John 4! Jesus is at Shechem *where there is no river*, and he is offering "living water!"

2. Revised edition, Geoffrey W. Bromiley, gen. ed., 4 vols. (Grand Rapids: Eerdmans, 1979–1988).

3. Buttrick, George A., gen. ed. *The Interpreter's Dictionary of the Bible: An Illustrated Encyclopedia*, 4 vols. (Nashville: Abingdon, 1962); Keith Crim, gen. ed., *Supplementary Volume, The Interpreter's Dictionary of the Bible* (Nashville: Abingdon, 1976).

4. For a list of these, see David M. Scholer, *A Basic Bibliographic Guide for New Testament Exegesis*, 2d ed. (Grand Rapids: Eerdmans, 1973), 26–30.

There are other basic tools, though, that will open to us the literary world of the Gospel of John. Written by well-known researchers, they are designed to be used by scholars and students who are seeking a digest of concepts and ideas from antiquity.

Four Reference Tools

There are four reference tools whose value to New Testament exegesis is so established that Bible students usually need only refer to them by an acrostic abbreviation. In each case they anchor their discussions in the Greek, but this does not make them inaccessible to those who must work in English.

(1) BAGD

A Greek-English Lexicon of the New Testament and Other Early Christian Literature, 2d ed. *(BAGD),*[5] is the premier lexicon for New Testament exegesis. Whenever a New Testament exegete seeks to translate a Greek word, understand its irregular forms, and trace its occurrences in the New Testament, *BAGD* is the volume of choice. Entries are listed alphabetically and then classified by use and meaning. A key is given to the completeness of the survey as well. If an entry is followed by one asterisk (*) this means that every reference to the word in the Greek literature surveyed by the lexicon (a considerable list) is provided. Two asterisks signify that all references in the New Testament are supplied.

Definitions in *BAGD* include comments about how the word is used in its literary context. For example, in John 3 Nicodemus is told that he must be born ἄνωθεν (*anōthen*). *BAGD* explains that this form is an adverb and lists three possible meanings, with references to similar grammatical constructions throughout the New Testament. Those meanings for ἄνωθεν are:

---

5. Walter Bauer, et al., *A Greek-English Lexicon of the New Testament and Other Early Christian Literature,* 2d ed., trans. William F. Arndt (Chicago: University of Chicago Press, 1979). Originally researched by Bauer, this volume was updated and translated by Arndt and Frederick W. Gingrich in 1957, and again most recently by Gingrich and Frederick W. Danker in 1979. The 2d ed. takes full advantage of current linguistic research and supplies references to major articles in *TDNT* (see below). The abbreviation *BAGD* honors authors Bauer, Arndt, Gingrich, and Danker.

1. Locally, from above
2. Temporally, (a) from the beginning, or (b) for a long time
3. Again or anew

Is Nicodemus being told that he must be born "from above," that is, from heaven? Or is this to be an experience that repeats something that happened before—he must be "born again?" The editors of *BAGD* are convinced that this is a classic example of Johannine double meaning, in which one word, through irony, conveys two meanings: If so it would mean both definitions one *and* three.[6]

Generally we find that in word research the definitions, with their references, are not enough. *BAGD* is a basic tool, but it is just a beginning. Theological dictionaries take us the next step further by examining root meaning and semantic background.[7]

(2) TDNT

The nine-volume *Theological Dictionary of the New Testament* (*TDNT*)[8] is an English translation of *Theologisches Wörterbuch zum Neuen Testament*, the famous German work edited by Gerhard Kittel and continued by G. Friedrich. A remarkable encyclopedia of Greek words and their history in antiquity, *TDNT* has no peer as a scholarly resource.[9]

---

6. Entries in *BAGD* at first appear confusing. References to nonbiblical texts are generally given first in parentheses. This is then followed by New Testament references. The Greek word is usually abbreviated; in our example using ἄνωθεν it appears as "ἄ.": Thus, the *BAGD* entry reads like this:

> 3. *again, anew.* (Pla., Ep. 2 p. 310ᴇ ἄ. ἀρξάμενος; Epict. 2, 17, 27; Jos., Ant. 1, 263; IG VII 2712, 58; BGU 595, 5ff) ἄ. ἐπιδεικνύναι MPol 1:1. Oft. strengthened by πάλιν, Gal 4:9—ἄ. γεννηθῆναι is purposely ambiguous and means both *born from above* and *born again* J 3:3,7 (ἄ. γεννᾶσθαι also Artem. 1,13. . . .).

7. A recent lexicon attempted to organize the vocabulary of the New Testament into categories called "semantic domains." Rather than organizing the words alphabetically, they are placed in 93 thematic groups or conceptual units to show how words relate to one another. Categories include such things as plants, kinship terms, memory and recall, festivals, time, etc. Thus under "think," (domain number 30) the student can compare the different nuances of νοέω, κατανοέω, and λογίζομαι as well as phrases like ἀναβαίνω ἐπί; καρδίαν (to arise in the heart [an idiom]). There is a second index volume which permits a reader to locate a Greek or English word without guessing at its domain. J. P. Louw and Eugene A. Nida, eds., *The Greek English Lexicon of the New Testament Based on Semantic Domains*, 2 vols. (New York: UBS, 1988).

8. Gerhard Kittel, *The Theological Dictionary of the New Testament*, 9 vols., trans. Geoffrey Bromiley (Grand Rapids: Eerdmans, 1964–1972).

9. Inevitably, any set that attempts to be this comprehensive will be criticized for omissions and biases. This has been the case with *TDNT* as well. Some have urged that its use of sources is selective and that its research, tied to specific Greek words, tends to obscure the

Until the mid-1970s locating words in "Kittel" (another nickname) could be frustrating. All entries are organized around root words. Thus, essays may include numerous terms that possess some semantic link. For instance, the essay for κακός (*evil*) also contains entries for the related words ἄκακος, κακία, κακόω, κακοῦργος, κακοήθεια, κακοποιέω, κακοποιός, ἐγκακέω, and ἀνεξίκακος. Searching for ἄκακο" requires finding the proper subentry under (κακός). Fortunately, in 1976 Ronald Pitkin completed an index (vol. 10) to solve these problems through indexes to English words, Greek keywords, Hebrew and Aramaic keywords, and even Scripture citations. Looking up ἄκακος in the index easily provides its volume and page number.

TDNT surveys the history and meaning of words, based on their cultural setting. Hence, a term is commonly explained initially with reference to classical Greek usage. Then the essay moves on to information about the word's Old Testament, Septuagint, Hellenistic Judaism, and New Testament history. Not all essays are arranged in this format, however, so to be certain of gleaning all pertinent information it is necessary to study the entire article.

A related reference work is available for those who would like to own and use *TDNT* but are awed by either its price or technical discussions. Bromiley (the original translator) edited the nine volumes down to a one-volume edition, *The Theological Dictionary of the New Testament, Abridged in One Volume.*[10] This volume employs the Greek but transliterates every word for the non-specialist. Thus, ἰάομαι (*to heal*) appears as *iaomai*. Discussions generally begin with a survey of the term or concept in antiquity (usually the Greek world), move to the Old Testament and Judaism, then give extensive attention to the New Testament. I looked up the entry "water" and found background discussions on Greek usage, the Old Testament, and Judaism, along with the New Testament, arranged according to the following outline:

---

larger *conceptual* framework that every word employs. While these criticisms—especially the latter—may be true, nevertheless, *TDNT* is an unparalleled resource for investigating antiquity. An essay in volume 10 (the index volume) explains the history of *TDNT* and begins with this telling line from Samuel Johnson (1709–1784): "Dictionaries are like watches; the worst is better than none, and the best cannot be expected to go quite true" (p. 613).

10. Grand Rapids: Eerdmans, 1985.

I. The world of antiquity
   A. Greek usage
   B. Meaning
      1. The flood
      2. The Dispenser of life
      3. Cleansing

II. The Old Testament and Jewish world
   A. Usage
   B. Meaning
      1. Literal Use
         a) Drinking water and irrigation
         b) The flood
         c) Cleansing
         d) Transferred usage

III. The New Testament
   A. Water literally and metaphorically
      1. The synoptic tradition
      2. The Johannine writings
         a) The flood in Revelation
         b) Drinking water in Revelation and John's
            Gospel
         c) Healing and cleansing water in John's Gospel
      3. 2 Peter 3:5–6
   B. Baptismal water
      1. The saying of the Baptist
      2. Water baptism and Spirit baptism
      3. Water symbolism

IV. The early church
   A. Water symbolism
   B. Rules about baptismal water
   C. Sanctifying
   D. Holy water

Just as in the longer version, so in the abridged *TDNT*, entries are organized following primary Greek stems. Thus under the entry for law, *"nomos"* (νόμος) can be found in transliterated form all related words: *anomia* (*lawlessness*, ἀνομία), *anomos* (*lawless*, ἄνομος), *ennomos* (*lawful*, ἔννομος), *nomikos* (*lawyer*, νομικός), etc. If we are looking for *anomia* there is no use looking at the beginning under "*A.*" The beginning of the one-volume edition offers an index of all Greek words, typed alphabetically with a reference to their entry page. These are some of the most helpful pages in the book.

A final note to English readers of "*Kittel.*" The one volume edition also provides an extensive index of English words on pages xx–xxxvi. If transliterated Greek is a problem, a word like *Lord/lord* can be found, even if you don't know that the Greek word is *kurios* (κύριος). Best of all, not only is the primary discussion of *Lord* listed, but other major uses are given as well: *Lord, come*, 563; *the Lord's*, 486; *Lord's Supper*, 143; *Our Lord is/has come*, 563; *to be lord*, 486; *to become lord*, 486; *to lord it*, 486.

(3) NIDNTT

The New International Dictionary of New Testament Theology (*NID-NTT*)[11] is also a translation of a German reference work,[12] but many students find it more serviceable than *TDNT*. While employing the Greek text throughout, it is simple to use, always providing transliterations and explanations that never assume the reader to be a Greek scholar. It is also easier to use since its relative brevity (three volumes) tends to eliminate the more obscure scholarly material in Kittel. It even offers a glossary to explain technical terms for the beginning student.

Further, the set is organized around concepts presented in English. For instance, *NIDNTT* offers an entry under the concept of *reconciliation*, heading the article with the English synonyms "Reconciliation, Restoration, Propitiation, Atonement."[13] After a short introduction the article then handles in turn each of the Greek terms that relate to this conceptual framework: ἀποκατάστασις, ἱλάσκομαι, and καταλλάσσω. Each subdivision of the article studies one Greek word, attending to its chronological development,

---

11. Colin Brown, gen. ed., 3 vols. (Grand Rapids: Zondervan, 1975).
12. Originally Lothar Coenen, Erich Beyreuther, and Hans Bietenhard, eds., *Theologisches Begriffslexikon zum Neuen Testament*, trans. and rev. C. Brown. David Townsley and Russell Bjork published a comprehensive index to Scripture citations in the *NIDNTT* called, *Scripture Index to the New International Dictionary of New Testament Theology: And Index to Selected Extra Biblical Literature* (Grand Rapids: Zondervan, 1985).
13. 3:145–77.

cultural differences between Hebrew and Greek ideas, and similar information.

One virtue of *NIDNTT*'s organization is that language does follow conceptual patterns. If, for example, I want to study *faith* in the New Testament, simply looking up the Greek word for faith, πίστις (*pistis*), is insufficient. The *NIDNTT* shows me that the concept in Greek, as in other languages, relates to a variety of nuances and synonyms. The biblical notion of *faith* or *believing* must include a study of πείθομαι (*peithomai*, "to persuade or convince") and πιστεύω (*pisteuō*, "to believe or trust").

NIDNTT supplies the researcher with remarkable bibliographies, lengthy lists of articles and books for further research after each entry. The bibliographies are organized in two parts. The first, generally listed as "(a)," provides all English language references. Section "(b)" lists foreign language references. Some readers glance at the bibliography, see three paragraphs of German, and close the book—leaving tremendous resources behind.

(4) EDNT

At publication of this book, *The Exegetical Dictionary of the New Testament* (*EDNT*) is a translation project still in the process of completion.[14] Originally the *Exegetisches Wörterbuch zum Neuen Testament*, this three-volume set will quickly become a favorite among students. It works as a combination Greek lexicon and theological dictionary. Entries are in Greek, along with helpful linguistic information (part of speech declensions, etc.). A transliteration follows for readers working in English. In abbreviated form the articles relay an amazing amount of data at a glance, including key Greek words with conceptual similarities and the number of occurrences of the word in the New Testament.[15] The discussion of background and meaning covers classical Greek, the Septuagint, post-Old-Testament Judaism, and Hellenism.

---

14. H. Balz and G. Schneider, eds., *The Exegetical Dictionary of the New Testament* (Grand Rapids: Eerdmans, 1990). At this writing, vol. 1 is available and vols. 2 and 3 are expected shortly.
15. If all New Testament occurrences are given, the entry is followed by an asterisk (*). Otherwise a word count is given and broken down by canonical book.

Brief bibliographical lists after each entry always note relevant materials in *TDNT* and *NIDNTT*. Therefore, these volumes will become the "first stop" in any word search since they give the range of meanings, extent of use, and the volume and page numbers of two major English-language reference volumes. The authors list books and journal articles they deem to be of major importance.

This is a practical set, designed primarily for students who want a lexicon and a substantial theological dictionary in one reference. Its contributors keep in mind that many serious students of the New Testament struggle with Greek. Volume 3 will include an extensive index of English words and their Greek equivalents for non-Greek readers.

Special Tools

The resources discussed above help with any New Testament study, including specialized work in the Gospel of John. Major sections of *TDNT*, for instance, devote comments to Johannine usage and meaning.

Other places, though, provide insights exclusively for the study of the Gospel and its vocabulary. Most technical grammars note unique features of Johannine style. Almost twenty pages of Nigel Turner's fourth volume of *A Grammar of New Testament Greek— Style*[16] study different characteristics of Johannine grammar and word usage.

Some book-length treatments examine the vocabulary and literary environment of the Fourth Gospel. Two frequently cited volumes are E. A. Abbott, *Johannine Vocabulary*[17] and E. K. Lee, *The Religious Thought of St. John*.[18] Lee, for example, gives lengthy treatments on such Johannine concepts as *word, world, light, flesh, glory, salvation, life, spirit,* and *water*.

---

16. Edinburgh: T. and T. Clark, vol. 4, 1976. The original two volumes were written by J. H. Moulton, whose name remains on all four books in the set, often called "Moulton's Grammar." Nigel Turner wrote volumes three and four.

17. London: A. and C. Black, 1905. E. A. Abbott wrote another volume of similar interest entitled *Johannine Grammar* (London: A. and C. Black, 1906). Although these are older volumes, nevertheless their worth has not diminished over the years.

18. London: SPCK, 1950.

Monographs and journal articles commonly provide creative thoughts. While these may have to be located through a careful bibliographical search (see chap. 6), their importance should not be minimized. If we are working on the word *spirit* or πνευςμα (pneuma) in John, we will be the poorer if we overlook H. S. Benjamin's article "*Pneuma* in John and Paul: A Comparative Study of the Term with Particular Reference to the Holy Spirit."[19] In this essay the author carefully analyzes each occurrence of pneuma in the Gospel, then does a theological comparison with similar themes in Paul. More specific still, assume we are interested in the concept of "Spirit and Truth" in John. There is a dissertation by R. E. Breck entitled "Spirit and Truth: A Study of the Background and Development of Johannine Pneumatology."[20] Specialized studies make a tremendous difference in any Johannine word study. But because they are so specialized, they require effort to locate. This is why the indexes discussed in chapter 6 are so helpful.

Finally, commentaries generally focus on words peculiar to John. Few students notice that at the end of volume 1 of Raymond E. Brown's commentary on John[21] an appendix surveys terms unique in the canon to John's Gospel, among them *truth, love, see, glory, commandment, life, world, remain, belief, darkness*, and *hour*. Lengthy independent treatments consider *the word, signs and works*, and *"I am"* in the Gospel. Appendixes at the end of volume 2 explore themes unique to the *Book of Glory* (John 13–21).

Other commentators tend to give specialized studies as well, but they are not as convenient. Rudolf Schnackenburg[22] provides more than one excursus on special words throughout his text and these must be tracked down with the help of the index or table of contents. The same is true of John Henry Bernard,[23] George R. Beasley-Murray,[24] and Leon Morris.[25]

All of these tools highlight the unique characteristics of the Fourth Gospel and sensitively interpret issues inherent to John. But they

19. *Biblical Theology Bulletin* 6 (1976): 27–48.
20. Ph.D. diss., Ruprecht-Karl Universität, Heidelberg, Germany, 1971.
21. Raymond E. Brown. *The Gospel According to John*, 2 vols. Anchor Bible Commentaries. (New York: Doubleday, 1966–1970).
22. *The Gospel According to St. John*, 3 vols., trans. K. Smyth (New York: Seabury, 1979).
23. *Critical and Exegetical Commentary on the Gospel of St. John*, ed. A. H. McNeile (London: T. and T. Clark, 1928).
24. *John* (Waco, Tex.: Word, 1987).
25. *Gospel of John* (Grand Rapids: Eerdmans, 1970).

should be used in conjunction with the other research volumes listed above. *NIDNTT* and *TDNT* are unmatched for thoroughness, especially when looking at the larger literary environment of the first century.

Common Johannine Word Study Errors

Anyone who sets out to study words in the New Testament is going to make mistakes. Linguistics is a difficult field and even though each of us feels confident with the use and meaning of words, still, deciphering *ancient words* presents special problems.

Many scholars have outlined the pitfalls that await unwary exegetes, and it is unnecessary to repeat all their warnings here.[26] Nevertheless, a handful of blunders recur with such frequency that we would do well to note them.

(1) The Root Error[27]

The Greek language often forges one word from a composite of two or three other terms. Students, therefore, can dissect words and look at the meaning of each individual part. Also, new words may be built from older words, and exegetes frequently claim dramatic new insights after digging into a word's etymological family tree.

The chief problem is that no word is equal to the sum of its parts. Anthony C. Thiselton notes that the English *person* originated in the Latin *persona*, meaning "mask." But is mask the *real* meaning? Does *person* in English have anything to do with *mask* in common speech? When we say "Good-bye," do we *really mean* "God be with you" (the origin of the phrase)?[28] On the contrary,

---

26. See esp. Anthony C. Thiselton, "Semantics and New Testament Interpretation," in *New Testament Interpretation: Essays on Principles and Methods*, I. Howard Marshall, ed. (Grand Rapids: Eerdmans, 1977), 75–104; D. A. Carson, *Exegetical Fallacies* (Grand Rapids: Baker, 1984), 25–90; Darrell Bock, "New Testament Word Analysis," in Scott McKnight, ed., *Introducing New Testament Interpretation* (Grand Rapids: Baker, 1989), 110–13; Moises Silva, *Biblical Words and their Meaning: An Introduction to Lexical Semantics* (Grand Rapids: Zondervan, 1983), and idem, *God, Language and Scripture: Reading the Bible in Light of General Linguistics* (Grand Rapids: Zondervan, 1991).

27. This is often called "the etymological error."

28. Thiselton, "Semantics," 80–81. Thiselton observes that *hussy* comes from *housewife*, but anyone who uses the terms interchangeably does so at some risk!

common sense tells us that words evolve. As Thiselton says, "the etymology of a word is *not a statement about its meaning but about its history.*"[29]

The same is true with Greek. It is incorrect to examine the history of a word and conclude that we now know its meaning. For instance, "to show compassion" is conveyed with the word σπλαγχνίζομαι (*splagxnizomai*). But this has little to do with "inner organs or intestines" (σπλάγχνα). The original thought dissipated with time and a new idea emerged. Similarly in English when I say "losing heart" I rarely have in mind some cardiac emergency. This has become an idiom and must be treated accordingly.

In the Fourth Gospel there is a notorious misuse of the term for the Holy Spirit, παράκλητος (*paraklētos*). It is made up of the two words παρά (*para*, "alongside or by") and καλέω (*kaleō*, "to call"). And it often is interpreted as "one who is called alongside of someone in need." This may be the history of the word, but it is another matter to say this is what John signifies in chapters 14–16 when he describes the Spirit. Had this become a conventional word, a familiar word whose root meanings were obscure?[30] Exegesis must discover what words mean when they are used as wholes in their own setting.

(2) The Anachronism Error

It is a commonplace to say that words change meaning over time. This means two errors always threaten an interpretation: First, meanings that evolved late may be read *back* into words used in earlier contexts. Second, ancient meanings may be read *forward* into more recent contexts. In the classic example of anachronistic use of New Testament Greek an expositor explains that the Greek word for *miracle* is δύναμις (*dynamis*) and then notes its connection with the modern word *dynamite*. Then the exposition goes on to trans-

---

29. Ibid, 81; emphasis added.
30. I once had the chore of studying the complete history of this word and its Johannine meaning. It was sobering to see how often linguistics are misused. Expositors today aggravate the problem when they note that some translations call the Paraclete "the Comforter;" then they refer to the Latin origin of "comforter" as "one who strengthens" (Lat., *confortare*, "to strengthen"). Thus, they say (coming full circle), Paraclete means "one who strengthens or fortifies!" The chain ends up looking like this: Paraclete=Comforter=*confortare*="One who makes strong."

late all New Testament uses of δύναμις as if they meant *dynamite*. Romans 1:16 brings sadly humorous sermonizing: "I am not ashamed of the gospel, for it is the *dynamite* of God unto salvation for everyone who believes." We are left to reflect on the explosive nature of the gospel.[31] This sort of exegesis just will not do.

Another example is the English word *martyr*, etymologically related to the Greek μάρτυς (*martys*, to bear witness). Does every reference to witnessing in the New Testament carry with it the notion of martyrdom? Not at all. The *subsequent history* of this word changed as church history learned the result of witnessing in a hostile world.

Neither the history of a word nor its later uses can be the key to meaning, any more than a word's component parts can be the key. Meaning is derived from a word's use in its *own chronological context*. John's careful theological use of λόγος (*logos*, "word"), for example, must be determined, not by use in classical Greek literature that preceded the Gospel by hundreds of years, but by analogies contemporary to the writing.

(3) The Prescriptive Error

An author may use the same word several times while writing a single manuscript but communicate through these uses a variety of meanings. Finding the meaning of a word in one passage, the exegete should not conclude that the same definition fits all other uses. Such a conclusion usually errs, as it "prescribes" meaning for the entire book based on one occurrence.

This happens frequently in the Fourth Gospel. For example, John clearly infers theological symbolism when he talks about *water*, as in 7:37–39 and 19:34. In these passages, water likely refers to the Spirit Jesus in his ministry now offers. But we have already seen that *water* can relate to a number of other meanings in John. Sacramental interpreters quickly see symbolism in every use of "water," automatically connecting each to renewal or baptism. But this limits John's flexibility. Literary environments within a book—or even within a chapter of scripture—must be seen as fluid in their use of individual words.

---

31. This example is noted in Carson, *Exegetical Fallacies*, 32–33.

A flagrant example of the prescriptive error haunts interpretations of Jesus' "I am" (ἐγώ ἐιμι, *ego eimi*) declarations. Certainly
John applies this form in an absolute sense to a connection between
Jesus and God's divine name (for example, in 8:24, 28, 58; 13:19). In
each of these statements the verb has no predicate (as it does in
6:35, 48, 51; 8:12; 10:7, 9, 11, 14; 11:25; 14:6; 15:1, 5). However, does
this mean that every use of "I am" which lacks a predicate establishes the same result? Sometimes Jesus is simply identifying himself (8:18, 23; 14:3). Sometimes it is unclear. When he is arrested in
the garden, 18:5–8 says that, upon hearing his words ἐγώ ἐιμι, the
arresting party fell back to the ground. Is this a theophany? Is the
power of the divine name being revealed? That may well be the
case, but the point cannot be made simply by arguing from other
uses of ἐγώ ἐιμι without a predicate. Each case must be studied
carefully on its own.

(4) Johannine Variation and Unnecessary Nuances

Every writer uses synonyms. This was no less true among the
ancient writers. And yet when we read modern writing we do not
stop to analyze supposed differences in nuance between two similar verbs or nouns. Usually the author is simply using variation as
a literary technique. A new verb adds new interest to a sentence
without necessarily conveying new meanings.

Exegetes forget this when they analyze why John changes verbs
or nouns, even in the same sentence. Turner describes John as having "pointless variety in style."[32] The Fourth Gospel supplies two
words each for the English words *love, send, heal, ask, speak, do, feed,
sheep, know*, sometimes with no apparent reason—except to avoid
monotony. This is especially true of the selection of prepositions.
Philip is ἀπό Bethsaida but ἐκ the city of Andrew (1:44). Lazarus
was ἀπό Bethany but ἐκ the village of Mary (11:1). This curiosity of
Johannine style appears both in the Gospel and the epistles and
must be considered in any exegesis.

This becomes an important issue when Bible students propose
that some Johannine variation infers something significant exeget-
ically. In John 21:15–17 Jesus carries on a discussion with Peter

32. Nigel Turner, *A Grammar of New Testament Greek*, Vol. 4, *Style* (Edinburgh: T. and T.
Clark, 1976), 76–77. See further W. F. Howard, *The Fourth Gospel in Recent Criticism and Interpretation*, 4th ed., rev. C. K. Barrett (London: Epworth, 1955), 276–96.

concerning love. Ἀγαπάω (agapaō, to love) and φιλέω (phileō, to love) are used in the following manner:

Round 1: Jesus: ἀγαπάω; Peter: φιλέω.
Round 2: Jesus: ἀγαπάω; Peter: φιλέω.
Round 3: Jesus: φιλέω; Peter: φιλέω.

Is it correct to suggest that this is Johannine wordplay, intended to underscore a subtle theological message? Or is this simply Johannine variation, treating two verbs as simple synonyms? Exegetes must be cautioned against running after new meanings where none exist.

(5) Respecting the Johannine Context

When I examine a word in any book of Scripture I must permit the author to establish the word's meaning—even a meaning unique to that passage—by context. The theological setting created by the author provides the significance of a word's communicated message. Particularly in regard to John, a meaning that a word may have in other books should not be automatically presumed to apply.

The Fourth Gospel uses many words exactly as, say, Paul might use them. The Johannine vocabulary for *belief* (πιστεύω, etc.) is similar to that of Paul. But there are instances where John is using a word with a meaning that is entirely his own. And in cases such as these, word study which draws in meaning from other contexts will obscure the intended meaning of the Fourth Gospel.

Some examples will make this clear. John uses the Greek word ὑψόω (hypsoō, to lift up) in a specialized way. The word is generally used by Paul and Luke to mean "exaltation," in particular, Jesus' exaltation to heaven in his resurrection/ascension (Phil. 2:9; Acts 2:33; 5:31). But John uses the word with a double sense in every passage where it occurs (see 3:14; 8:28; 12:32, 34). Ὑψόω also means Jesus' "lifting up on the cross" (just as the serpent was lifted up in the wilderness, 3:14). The cross in Johannine theology is a place of glorification, just as heaven will be.[33]

A similar confusion surrounds John's use of δοξάζω (doxazō, to glorify). In most of the New Testament the word describes the

---

33. A complete study of ὑψόω can be found in *TDNT* 8:610.

glory of Jesus in his resurrection—a vindication of his sonship after the crucifixion (1 Tim. 3:16; 1 Cor. 2:8). In the Synoptic Gospels it is connected with Christ's second coming or parousia (Mark 8:38; 10:37, etc.) or in Luke, it is linked with the birth and transfiguration of Jesus (Luke 2:9; 9:32). But nowhere is δόξα a common feature of Jesus' earthly life. John's gospel is different. Not only is δόξα used to describe the revelation of God in Jesus' ministry, but δοξ- άζω points forward, not just to the resurrection, but also to the time of the denial, the trial, and the cross. Thus in 13:31 Jesus says, "Now the Son of Man has been glorified!" Δοξάζω is already underway! In Johannine theology, glorification refers to all of the events of passion week.[34]

This may seem like an unimportant distinction until we read a verse like 7:39, "for as yet there was no Spirit because Jesus was not yet glorified." Spirit must await glorification. But when does this occur? In John 20:22 we find the very difficult description of the resurrected Jesus breathing on the disciples and saying, "Receive the Holy Spirit." Has 7:39 been fulfilled? Is glorification finished? Has it even begun? Our interpretation of δόξα as a Johannine theological concept will determine the answer for us.

Conclusion

Interpretation is a discipline that requires a number of carefully developed skills if it is to be successful. Students of Scripture should be fully prepared to employ the very best research tools available to unlock the meaning of the texts that have come down to us through the centuries. Concordances, dictionaries, journal articles, and commentaries exist to help us accomplish one thing: discern the original meaning of a passage *so that* we might benefit from it ourselves or carry its message to others.

This brings us to our final subject. Interpretation is not an end in itself. Historical research, diagramming sentences, combing through *TDNT*, and becoming a friend of *New Testament Abstracts* are all useful exercises only if they result in a message that can be preached. Exegesis is preparation, a prelude. Its test is in what we hear from the pulpit.

---

34. Scripture quotations from NRSV.

Preaching and Exegesis from the Fourth Gospel

Introduction to Part 4

The other day I pulled from my files the first notes I took in seminary. My first class met on September 30, 1974, with Robert Munger, whose challenge was to teach his fledgling seminarians about "the foundations of ministry." First day . . . first class . . . first notes . . . I paged through that file, curious to see what I had written now that many years had elapsed.

Dr. Munger asked us what we expected to do with our lives once we were graduated from Fuller Theological Seminary. After three years of studying exegesis, church history, pastoral counseling, homiletics, and theology we would have plenty of "stuff" to tell people in the church!

Then he surprised us by announcing that *all of our knowledge would be useless unless we learned to use these tools to bring spiritual truths to the people we would be called to lead!* To be effective both our lives and our words would have to proclaim what we learned from the study of Scripture.

That same week of beginnings I read Samuel M. Shoemaker's little volume, *Beginning Your Ministry*.[1] Shoemaker said the same thing: Evangelical seminaries can have the peculiar liability of producing young scholars who can exegete a text as an exercise in historical research, but find themselves unable to turn the text into a meaningful sermon. *Exegesis is simply a vehicle meant to take us somewhere else.* It is never an end in itself. If it does not lead to a message that feeds, inspires, convicts, and nourishes God's people, it is worthless in our repertoire of ministry tools.

---

1. New York: Harper and Row, 1963; repr. ed., Pasadena, Calif.: Fuller Theological Seminary, n.d.

Preaching from the Gospel of John is a privilege. This book is the beloved gospel of the church; people welcome its exposition. Everywhere I have used the Fourth Gospel—in college lectures, chapel homilies, or sermons—the response is the same. John is a comfortable Gospel, a familiar, dear friend to the laity.

On the one hand, this means people are eager listeners and learners in the presence of this Gospel. Their hearts are receptive to its message. On the other hand, this also means people have brought certain expectations with them. They assume what they hear will be important and profound and inspiring because John's Gospel has proven its power in their lives.

Therefore, the relationship between exegesis and preaching is always central, but chapters 10 and 11 are singularly crucial; how can all the discoveries gleaned from commentaries, concordances, and elsewhere translate into a meaningful message?

10

The Problem of Horizons

Today's interpreters understand that Scripture inhabits a setting utterly foreign to the modern life of the church. Its culture lives on one horizon, we on another. Imagine looking at the Bible as if it were a distant, mysterious panorama and two thousand years removed. For all its familiarity and clarity, John still comes from an historical setting remote from our own. Sometimes Western readers think we understand when in fact we do not, for we misapprehend subtle differences in how human writers of Scripture understood culture, language, history, and theology. As tourists at a scenic vista, we know where we are, but only gaze at the distant landscape and wonder what it is like there. We interpret from afar.

This science of interpretation—called hermeneutics[1]—spawned lively debate during the 1900s. Some features of this debate affect those of us who wish to bring the Fourth Gospel into the pulpit. The people in the pews likewise experience the problem of "distance" from the Word of God. They struggle to find meaning in these ancient foreign stories.

Where does *meaning* reside? Is the meaning of John 6 something objective in the mind of the fourth evangelist? Is it locked into the

---

1. Hermeneutics derives from the Gk. ἑρμηνεύω (*hermēneuō*, to interpret or explain), ἑρμη-νεία (*hermēneia*, translation or interpretation), and ἑρμηνευτής (*hermēneutēs*, a translator of foreign tongues). Peter Cotterell and Max Turner define hermeneutics as "the study of how we determine what a discourse means. By 'discourse' we mean any form of oral or written communication; from a legal summons to Tennyson's 'The Lady of Shalott,' and from the snatch of an utterance in Acts 5:30 . . . to the whole of Acts." In *Linguistics and Biblical Interpretation* (Downers Grove, Ill.: Inter-Varsity, 1989), 53.

sentences and paragraphs of that chapter? Is the meaning of John something that resides in the "far horizon," continually challenging interpreters to undertake the quest of retrieving it? If this is the case, interpreters work as detectives, employing every skill at their disposal to discover the *original* meaning.

On the other hand, numerous philosophers and theologians have argued that meaning resides instead *in the perception and experience of the interpreter.* Truth is experiential—something that changes us, something that becomes authentic when it impacts our lives. It is not a relic in some distant treasure box we have to dust off and open. Instead it is living and active, a "two-edged sword." The meaning of John 6 is found in *what I discover there.* The meaning of John 6 is *what God says to me as I read it.* One minister I know is fond of saying from the pulpit before Scripture is read, "Listen *for* the Word of God," instead of "Listen *to* the Word of God." For him the words of the Bible are not intrinsically God's words that we are called to *listen to;* as we respond they *become* God's words.

At a workshop on self-portraits for children at Chicago's Institute of Fine Arts, the teacher took my family on a tour of famous paintings in the galleries. One picture in particular captured my attention. It showed a young painter in a Dutch landscape with his tools arranged on a table around him. "What is this work's value?" I wondered. "What is its *meaning* as it sits on the wall? Why do we regard it as worthwhile?"

For our teacher, an art historian, the self-portrait represented primary evidence of a particular historical period. Its style, its colors, even its message, was historical: "Look what we can learn about the sixteenth century!" Frankly, I didn't care about all of the brilliant details he so carefully explained. The minutiae were a distraction. The painting seemed message aplenty. As if the canvas had words, a young man spoke to me through the centuries about the pride he took in his work, the excellence of his craftsmanship, and his devotion. I now know more about that painting's historical background, but whenever I return to the Institute and see this painting, *its meaning will remain the same for me.* It is a contemporary, timeless message, which only I can know, but which, if I try, I can share with others. *For me it is the only significant message that comes from the canvas.*

If it is true that for this painting "meaning" resides on my *near horizon*—my present consciousness and experience—why can't the same be true of literature? Literary critics have been making this point for years, calling it "reader-response criticism." An English professor whom I know well contends that any other way to interpret literature today is *passé*. A poem can mean one thing to one reader and quite another to a second reader. Interpretation, therefore, involves personal experience, and meaning changes, depending on who is doing the reading.

Take one example. Poems and paintings and books have no meaning unless they correspond to something that already exists in our minds.[2] Experiences give meaning to what we see and hear. If someone gives me a piece of wood and a piece of steel, I only know that it is a broken hammer because I have used hammers before. *Hammer* is something I recognize. This correct interpretation comes from within, not just from the wood and steel. I am an active agent in this interpretative process.

But what about when we are exposed to something for which no previous knowledge or experience can be found to draw upon? I cannot interpret some technical articles about computers, no matter how clearly they are written. No analogies to their metaphors or images exist in my mind. C. S. Lewis was getting at this in his "space trilogy" when his hero, Ransom, steps onto the planet Malacandra (Mars) and sees things he cannot explain:

> He gazed about him, and the very intensity of his desire to take in the new world at a glance defeated itself. He saw nothing but colours—colours that refused to form themselves into things. *Moreover he knew nothing yet well enough to see it: you cannot see things until you know roughly what they are.* His first impression was of a bright, pale world—a watercolour world out of a child's paint-box.[3]

Like Ransom we struggle for meaning when our experiences cannot connect with what we encounter. In Ezekiel 1:26–28 the prophet tries to describe the glory of the Lord, but it is evident that words cannot contain the images he finds.

Is the same true for biblical literature? Is it true for the Gospel of John? Have we defined ourselves as historians of antiquity—

---

2. This is known in hermeneutics as our *preunderstanding*.
3. C. S. Lewis, *Out of the Silent Planet* (N. Amer. ed., New York: Macmillan, 1952), 46.

explaining images and ideas to people who cannot comprehend? Like Nicodemus in John 3, is the substance of Jesus' discourses so foreign as to be incomprehensible?

The Problem of Theological Education

James D. Smart describes how this acute problem for the minister has been created in part by our seminaries.[4] Biblical and practical theology curricula have been divorced, as have homiletics and hermeneutics. Students cultivate technical exegetical skills in one quarter and work on techniques of preaching in another. Because seminaries fall victim to specialization, students who someday will enter the pulpit find themselves at a severe disadvantage. I recall wondering how the outstanding exegetical lessons of Ralph P. Martin and George E. Ladd would be useful since homiletics professors used few if any of these skills. Of what use is a critical Greek commentary on John if no sermon really needs it? Worse, few courses hone skills in using the Bible in the pulpit. Smart writes:

> Many preachers today feel themselves trapped and imprisoned in an intolerable situation in regard to the Bible. They are bound by their vows and their tradition to a book that is more of a burden to them than an infinite resource. Not more than 5 percent of it has been useful to them in their preaching and teaching. And yet they are expected to preach from it and teach it incessantly. In seminary their training in exegesis was concentrated upon textual, literary, and historical problems. They learned to place the text in its original historical situation and to hear it with the accents of the ancient speaker or author. They had a general introduction to each of the testaments as a whole. They were made familiar with a vast variety of problems with which the Scriptures confront the scholar and the even vaster variety of solutions to those problems which across the years have been devised by the scholars. But at two points they are unlikely to remember much in their seminary training that is a help to them: on how to get from the original meaning of a text in its ancient situation to the meaning of the same text in a late twentieth-century world, or on how to deal honestly and adequately with

---

4. James D. Smart, *The Strange Silence of the Bible in the Church: A Study in Hermeneutics* (Philadelphia: Westminster, 1970), 28–38.

the critical problems generated by the Biblical text when they confront the rudimentary educational milieu of a local congregation.[5]

Without the skill to bring the Bible into the twentieth century, preachers pass along to laypeople the impression that the Bible belongs on the relic heap. Witness the absence of genuine expository preaching in most American pulpits. Even evangelical preachers who think that they are anchoring their message in "the text" do quite the opposite. After the preacher reads and briefly explains the passage, the text becomes only a launching pad for some contemporary pastoral issue. Sometimes these pastoral homilies retain the barest link to the passage. The preacher lacks even an awareness that this approach fails to bridge the hermeneutical gulf.

Where do hermeneutics and homiletics meet in such an environment—or will they ever join, given the insurmountable obstacles separating them? Anthony C. Thiselton identifies the key question as "how the New Testament may speak to us *anew*. A literalistic repetition of the text cannot *guarantee* that it will 'speak' to the modern hearer."[6]

The New Hermeneutic

Those who have champion a new way to look at the Bible offer one answer. Its roots go back to Martin Heidegger's existentialism; now it flourishes under the name the "new hermeneutic."[7] Karl Barth and Rudolf Bultmann pioneered its modern expression in the 1920s and 1930s. Barth studied under some of the best exegetical minds in Europe, yet he discovered his exegetical skills were of no use to him as he served in a Swiss pastorate. Barth

---

5. Ibid, 29.

6 Anthony C. Thiselton, "The New Hermeneutic," in I. Howard Marshall, ed., *New Testament Interpretation: Essays on Principles and Methods* (Grand Rapids: Eerdmans, 1977), 309.

7. The new hermeneutic has generated an immense pool of scholarly writing. A classic presentation of the movement by its proponents is James M. Robinson and John B. Cobb, eds., *The New Hermeneutic* (New York: Harper and Row, 1964). Some of the best critiques can be found in Smart, *Strange Silence*, and Thiselton, "The New Hermeneutic." See also the thorough study by Thiselton, *The Two Horizons: New Testament Hermeneutics and Philosophical Description, with Special Reference to Heidegger, Bultmann, Gadamer, and Wittgenstein* (Grand Rapids: Eerdmans, 1980). This revision of Thiselton's Ph.D. dissertation contains a significant bibliography (pp. 447–66). An American evangelical who has written at length on the new hermeneutic is Royce G. Gruenler of Gordon-Conwell Seminary. See his *Meaning and Understanding: The Philosophical Framework for Biblical Interpretation* (Grand Rapids: Zondervan, 1990).

experimented with a fresh view of the Bible. The stir he began when, in 1919, he published his commentary on Romans continues even now.[8] For Barth, revelation does not happen when we study the Bible, as if it were a laboratory object under our microscopes. Rather it happens when we let the Bible study us. *When we become the objects of its enquiry, when we become listeners—then God speaks!* We don't discover the message, the message discovers us. Therefore, revelation happens in the twentieth century—not just in the first century!

Barth was not a professional New Testament exegete, so many disregarded his criticisms, until they were echoed ten years later by Bultmann. In 1934 his popular address to students, "How Does God Speak to Us Through the Bible?" made the following remarks:

> "How does God speak to us through the Bible?" Who asks that? Would someone who is certain *that* God speaks through the Bible ask such a question? Why should he want to know *how*? If it were asked as a purely theoretical question, it would be a useless, even a frivolous game. For what God says to us through the Bible is in the form of an *address*. It can only be listened to, not examined. The man to whom God really speaks through the Bible hears what God says to him and acts accordingly, and he has just as little time and reason to ponder over the *how*, as has a son to submit the style of his father's words to theoretical examinations. In doing so, he would forget to hear rightly.[9]

Hearing *rightly* is the concern of the new hermeneutic. Barth complained that New Testament scholars had become historians—not theologians. As a result, their message had become meaningless. Bultmann took a more text-critical approach: The New Testament texts themselves contained inappropriate and incomprehensible archaic language and thought forms. These forms—called *myths*—had to be eliminated so that the New Testament message could be heard anew.[10]

---

8. *Römerbrief*, E.T. E. C. Hoskyns from the 6th ed., *Epistle to the Romans* (London: Oxford University Press, 1933).

9. "How Does God Speak to Us Through the Bible?" in Rudolf Bultmann, *Existence and Faith: The Shorter Writings of Rudolf Bultmann*, S. M. Ogden, trans. and ed. (New York: World, 1960), 166. Originally the lecture appeared in *The Student World* 27 (1934): 108–12. Bultmann's writings in this area are numerous and often technical. See an extensive bibliography in Thiselton, *Two Horizons*.

10. This explains Bultmann's program of "demythologization." It was *not* an attempt to discredit the Christian faith, but to hear the Bible *rightly*, to unlock the message that was shrouded in the history and culture and the so-called "superstition" of first-century life.

Today the heirs of this view—especially Ernst Fuchs, Robert W. Funk, Gerhard Ebeling, and Hans Georg Gadamer—share three primary affirmations:[11]

1. They reject a "spectator hermeneutic" in which the Bible becomes a relic of archeology for the exegete to analyze. There is a subjective element to all interpretation, they affirm, so revelation takes place only as the interpreter *engages the text* and listens. Antiquarian research is of dubious value. What scripture *says to me* is more important than what scripture *said two thousand years ago.*
2. They urge that interpretation is incomplete until the message of the text confronts the present era. Any author, any preacher, any teacher who simply lays out *what the passage meant in the first century* misses the primary purpose of making sense of the Bible so that it speaks today.
3. Their central point is that *revelation is a transforming event* in which God comes to us in judgment or mercy, freeing us to be who he intended us to be. Lives are not changed through history lessons. An event of revelation and transformation through Scripture is inaccessible to the most careful historian and cannot be reconstructed through lexicons and grammars.

Assessment

Evangelicals quickly take up arms against this approach since it clearly places the locus of revelation in the experience of the believer rather than in Scripture. They feel that the authority of the Bible has been compromised. Yet we cannot dismiss the new hermeneutic until we see that it reminds us of something valuable: The Bible does have unique power when we can say "This passage has spoken personally to me." We know very well that experience is the gateway to transformation.

---

11. To sample these seminal thinkers see Gerhard Ebeling, *The Nature of Faith,* R. G. Smith, ed. (E.T., Philadelphia: Fortress, 1967); idem, *The Study of Theology,* trans. P. A. Duane (Ann Arbor, Mich.: Books on Demand, n.d.); Ernst Fuchs, *Studies of the Historical Jesus,* trans. A. Scobie (Naperville, Ill.: A. R. Allenson, 1964); Robert W. Funk, *Language, Hermeneutic and the Word of God: The Problem of Language in the New Testament and Contemporary Theology* (New York: Harper and Row, 1966); idem, *Parables and Presence: Forms of New Testament Tradition* (Philadelphia: Fortress, 1982), and Hans Georg Gadamer, *Truth and Method* (E.T., New York: Crossroad, 1982).

However, two primary problems beset the new hermeneutic: First, when we focus on our inner voice, we risk losing the original voice of Scripture, the historic anchor that has given the church its foundation and faith, and the uniqueness of a moment of historical revelation without parallel to anything we may experience. And elevating our own experience risks confusing what is subjectively true for me with what is objectively true. Truth resides in my own temporal experience.[12] Second, proponents of the new hermeneutic want to read the New Testament more deeply to understand its message powerfully. But do they want to understand the New Testament correctly? While exegesis risks becoming a discipline removed from the demands of the pulpit, so homiletics cannot separate itself from hermeneutics. That would power the pulpit by personal inspiration instead of by historical, critical study of the Bible. Hermeneutics and homiletics must remain wed. The relevance of the biblical message will not be rediscovered simply by jettisoning the traditional place of Scripture.

Where does that leave us? Historical exegesis alone is insufficient if it leaves the preacher without the tools for a sermon; new approaches to homiletics abandon the historic message of the New Testament text. Both options fall short. Henry J. Cadbury, the great Quaker New Testament scholar (1883–1974) recognized these temptations in his own generation. When some called for dismantling the historic New Testament record so a contemporary voice could be heard, he wrote a book called *The Peril of Modernizing Jesus*.[13] When some among the conservatives urged that the ancient *kerygma* or preaching of the early church alone would suffice, he published an article, "The Peril of Archaizing Ourselves."[14]

We need a hermeneutic that enables us to bridge the horizons. We need to draw from the far horizon that message as understood two thousand years ago—and we need to carry it into the twentieth century to nurture vital and relevant faith for our people today.

---

12. At the time of this writing a classic example of this conception had surfaced in the Presbyterian Church, U.S.A. Publication of the findings of a denominational taskforce on human sexuality became national news because the committee rejected biblical authority altogether and embraced virtually any form of "responsible sex" (among high school students, single people, gays, etc.). Contemporary experience and the behavioral sciences, they felt, deemed these practices to be morally neutral. In June 1991 the PCUSA General Assembly overwhelmingly rejected the report.

13. Henry J. Cadbury, *The Peril of Modernizing Jesus* (New York: MacMillan, 1937).

14. *Interpretation: A Journal of Bible and Theology* 3 (1949): 331–37.

Contextualization

Contextualization recently joined the growing list of technical words in the vocabulary of hermeneutics. Interest in contextualizing the gospel reflects a growing awareness among interpreters today that, as Richard Muller explains, "the gospel message arose in one cultural, social, historical, and linguistic context, and we live in another."[15] In order for the gospel to have meaning we need to bear it out of its native context and carry it into the cultural, social, historical, and linguistic context of our own day. The gospel needs to be contextualized *for us*.

This process is hardly new. The New Testament itself bears witness to the reformulation of doctrines from the Palestinian to the Greek setting of the church. The christologics of Matthew and Colossians bear eloquent testimony to this process at work. The process continued as theology moved from the Greek speaking church to the West. Contextualization has always been "one of the basic elements of the life, spread, and survival of Christianity."[16]

What distinguishes our era is that this process happens *consciously*. We have been awakened to the broad, international diversity of the church and rightly challenge the "westernization" of theology. Missionaries often have been as imperialistic as the colonists they preceded; to our shame third-world cultures have been forced to dress in western theological attire in order to be deemed "orthodox."

But if legitimate theologies spring from divergent cultures, a theological core must be at their base, a heart adaptable to new settings without losing the essentials. In Asia and particularly sub-Sahara Africa such authentic contextualization has achieved marked success in reformulating the gospel around forms completely different from those in the West. Contextualization succeeds when pastors and scholars build bridges between the world of the Bible and their own culture.

No easy formula governs this process. "Anytime that theology crosses a cultural boundary, whether historical or geographical,

---

15. Richard Muller, *The Study of Theology: From Biblical Interpretation to Contemporary Formulation* in vol. 7, Foundations of Contemporary Interpretation (Grand Rapids: Zondervan, 1991), 201. I am indebted to Muller for much that follows.
16. Ibid, 202.

new terms and new metaphors must be drawn out of the spiritual, intellectual, and linguistic storehouse of the culture and adapted for use in Christian theology."[17] This takes creative effort faithful both to the new culture and to the original biblical message.

Those most effective in this work are people native to the receiving culture who so thoroughly know the foreign culture that they can build bridges between the two. The apostle Paul is one example of a man who successfully brought the gospel from one culture (Judaism) to his native Hellenism. Contextualization continued as the gospel moved from Hellenism to the Latin West.[18]

In fact, the process of contextualization takes place regularly in any Christian ministry. Whenever someone preaches a sermon, prays for the sick, or explains the gospel to a group of college students, the message is being shaped by the context in which it is spoken. Christian ministry presupposes contextualization, making the task of the exegete-preacher a cross-cultural assignment. Without a conscious effort at contextualization, ministers find themselves reciting what went on in the biblical culture or discovering pastoral messages that spring from our own native culture. But neither alternative will do.

So successful preaching takes place when we carefully build a bridge between the biblical world and our own. This means we cannot simply give a dramatic recitation of what a story like John 3 meant in John's day. Nor can we cut a word, a phrase or a thought in the story and rapidly shove it into some contemporary application. It does mean that we find a genuine message in the text, discern how it is contextualized for its own time and place, and recontextualize it for our parish. We may find a process at work in this effort:

(1) Understanding the Original Context

Good exegesis should present a clear idea of the message in its original historical context. We should be able to distill the text's

---

17. Ibid, 210.
18. Muller points to Tertullian as another hermeneutical "bridge builder" who successfully reformulated the gospel and, in so doing, developed the basic elements of western theology.

intent and explain what was going on in the first century. Consider John 7, which places Jesus at the Feast of Tabernacles in Jerusalem. Exegesis discerns the centrality of the temple for Jewish hope, Jesus' messianic fulfillment of the Tabernacles water symbolism, and the expectation that this promise would come to pass when Jesus was glorified and the Spirit given. *This is the original story in its original setting.* Can this story speak in the twentieth century?

(2) Grasping the Essential Message

I need to discover what lesson, what theological principle, what truth John 7 conveys. There may be a body of truths from which to select. *My aim is to unwrap the message from its cultural historic setting so that I can carry it to my congregation.* One theme of John 7 critiques Judaism's wish to satisfy its longing for God through a tremendous religious institution, the Temple. Jesus came to Judaism's rituals, upset them, and announced that God desires something different. In Christ God offers "drink" in a new, personal sense that discloses power and immediacy. The message: Jesus Christ confronts religious tradition and institutions that dare to replace God himself. *Jesus offers in reality what institutions provide only in form.*

(3) Bear the Message Home

Finally I work to discover how this message relates to my context. Anchored in history, truth lives and stands ready to speak to the twentieth century. My denominational tradition also builds religious institutions. We cultivate them with care and find that they do indeed meet religious needs after a fashion. But in the end the immediacy of God becomes lost in ceremonies, choirs, glass windows, and committees of church life. We too need Jesus Christ to interrupt our festivals and make us pause to consider whether we relish ceremonies about God more than our desire to know him personally. Do we want ceremonial water, or living water? Do we want tradition, or do we want the Holy Spirit?

Conclusion

Experimentation with this three-step outline in sermons has shown that congregations delight in the results. Not only do they understand a message that is anchored in the Bible, but they are witnessing biblical interpretation at work. If shown how, they can carry over these skills to personal devotional study.

I was in church when a friend leaned over to me after the sermon and whispered, "Why doesn't he just tell me what the Bible story means—then and today? That's all I want." Inspiring stories of faith, citations from Nathanael Hawthorne and G. K. Chesterton, pleas from logic, or insights from psychology never satisfy as much as does well-informed, expository preaching. But then again neither do historical recitations about the first century that leave our life and circumstances untouched. The excellent preacher is a bridge-builder able to connect both horizons with skill and wisdom.

11

Preaching from John

Everyone offers advice on how to preach. The staggering number of books on the subject suggests that pitfalls as well as tips circulate out there; and the more tips I gather, the greater my chance of success.

Donald Mitchell, a native of New Zealand and one of the greatest preachers I know, was the president of King College in Bristol, Tennessee from about 1979 until 1989. Dr. Mitchell passed along to me the "advice" Martin Luther penned in the sixteenth century for all prospective preachers:

Good preachers should have these qualities and virtues:

1. They should be able to teach in a right and orderly way.
2. They should have a good head.
3. They should be able to speak well.
4. They should have a good voice.
5. They should have a good memory.
6. They should know when to stop.
7. They should be sure of their material and be diligent.
8. They should stake body and life, goods and honor on it.
9. They should suffer themselves to be vexed and flayed by everybody.

Preaching from the Fourth Gospel—or any of the gospels—presents unique challenges, especially for those who have labored over the text and discovered exciting details from the Greek text or the culture of first-century Palestine.

In chapter 10 I urged that preaching not be limited either to historical recitation of the past nor a contemporary message without historic biblical mooring. Once we have arrived at what seems to be a message that springs from our text, we next ask how to go about building it into a sermon. How do we deliver a sermon that is biblically grounded and effectively contextualized to our own world? How do we unleash the power of the Gospel of John in the church? We begin by noting some preaching practices that keep John's power locked away from the congregation and the preacher.

Stifling John's Power

Wearing Exegesis on Your Sleeve

As a newly-ordained Presbyterian minister I served as interim pastor at a small church in Appalachian Tennessee. This was not difficult since church responsibilities fit well with my college teaching schedule. But since I only had begun to teach, I was enamored with the disciplines of "the academy." My congregation heard far too much about New Testament theology and interpretation. This church was nestled in a scenic valley where a number of outsiders had summer homes. When they came to church, everyone—including the preacher—noticed. At the start of one service I noticed that the famous Old Testament scholar, James Mays from Union Seminary in Richmond, was in the congregation. Panic set in. The sermon seemed too simple *for him*. Before I knew it my sermon was explaining how the traditions of the *halachah* of first-century Judaism affected the transmission of the Synoptics.

I'm not sure if Dr. Mays was impressed (he never came back), but the congregation in its wisdom realized what was going on: *I was preaching for my own ego rather than for the needs of the people.* My hard-won insights from Jewish literature were being flagged before my audience like so many credentials. Fortunately the people of East Tennessee are gracious, patient and wise—they never held such excesses against me.

Exegesis is the scaffolding of the building, not the building itself. When used correctly, exegesis becomes virtually invisible from inside the cathedral. I once listened to a preacher who enjoyed "lists" hammer out "Thirteen Things Paul Believed About Baptism." Most of the thirteen were collected from works by George R. Beasley-

Murray and Joachim Jeremias. By the time another of his sermons reached the eleventh reason Jesus fed the five thousand, the entire congregation was comatose! One of the most brilliantly researched sermons I ever heard explained seven background sources for the term *logos* in John 1. Delivered in a Pasadena, California, church, the sermon's explanation of stoicism greatly inspired Fuller Seminary professors in the audience, but it did little for the average family in the pew.

Technical exegesis leads ministers and scholars making primary contact with the text to new insights and inspiration, but it does not have to be paraded before our congregations. Greek words need not be spelled, or even pronounced, from the pulpit unless they serve a very important purpose. Any preacher who feels compelled to mention Werner G. Kümmel for added authority needs to dismantle his scaffolding of exegesis.

Most of the best insights concerning the Gospel of John will come from such thorough critical commentaries as Raymond E. Brown, Barnabas Lindars, C. K. Barrett, and Beasley-Murray. Because we are convinced of the importance of first-century gnosticism and similar issues, we are tempted to tell people all about them. The place for this is in seminaries, colleges, and some adult education courses, but rarely does it fit a sermon. Excellent students, vigorously committed to study and research, fall prey to this temptation after gathering enough research for a term paper and then spending it in one twenty-minute sermon.

Pursuing Ancient Arguments

These students also face another serious danger as preachers: They are apt to project their congregations into conflicts and dilemmas brought forward from the first century, particularly when developing messages from the Fourth Gospel. Scholars frequently write in their commentaries about issues with which the "Johannine community" allegedly wrestled. A classic case involves John 1:35–37 and 3:22–36, units which tell how John the Baptist encouraged his disciples to transfer their loyalty to Jesus. Virtually every commentary remarks about tensions that existed in the first century between followers of the Baptist and followers of Jesus (see, for example, Acts 19:1–7). Many writers also dissect John in search of *layers of text tradition* from the developing Johannine community. Each narrative becomes a sort of foil, a window that lets us view another world other than that of Jesus.

What do we do with this information? It no doubt helps to illumine the Gospel's text, but we have to ask about the usefulness of such debates for our listeners. Few people come to church to learn about the theological development of the first century; yet we still have to work responsibly with the texts. *The problem comes when we see these speculative, critical issues as the primary message and then seek to find meaning in them for today.* Nothing could be further from the mark, nor more deadening to the vitality of John's exciting story than scholarly reconstructions of John's editorial history.

Taking Text Out of Context

A couple of years ago I had the opportunity to visit Harvard University. I noticed carved words above the porch of a very old humanities building: "That they might have life and have it abundantly." I've seen the same words above the central gates to the American University of Beirut, Lebanon, and I imagine the motto has been adopted by many schools and other organizations. The curious problem is that everyone loves the saying but few cite it in full: "[Jesus said,] *I came* that they might have life and have it abundantly" (John 10:10). Some scholars at Harvard or the American University might be shocked to learn that their beloved saying does not refer to philanthropy or the humanities.

John's Gospel endowed the world with rich thoughts. Because of their precision and beauty, many precepts recorded by the fourth evangelist stand quite ably on their own:[1]

In him was life, and the life was the light of all people.

And the Word became flesh and dwelt among us, full of grace and truth.
Unless you are born again, you cannot see the kingdom of God.

---

1. Sample texts are the author's translation and include, in the order presented, John 1:4; 1:14; 3:3; 3:16; 3:21; 4:24; 11:25.

For God so loved the world that he gave his only Son, that whoever believes in him should not perish but have eternal life.

But whoever does what is true comes to the light, that it may be
clearly seen that his deeds have been wrought in God.

God is spirit and those who worship him must worship in spirit
and in truth.

I am the resurrection and the life.

Though many quickly recognize these expressive words, preachers must resist the temptation to adapt them to the contemporary
scene, disregarding their original intention. One minister read John
3, underscoring the importance of being "born again." He went on
to show how everyone is "reborn" each time a new moment of
enlightenment and growth comes into their lives. This is a nice
thought, but it has little to do with the original meaning of John 3.

Familiarity and its succinct character makes John the book of
the New Testament perhaps most frequently quoted out of context. Sadly, sermons launched with good intentions run aground
when speakers overlook the author's intentions.

Holding John From the Outside

George MacDonald once said that nothing is so deadening to
the Divine as to habitually deal with the *outside* of holy things.
MacDonald was describing an occupational liability of divinity
students, priests, and pastors. C. S. Lewis, in his autobiography,
Surprised by Joy, put it this way: "The problem of the pastorate is
that those who hold holy things too often soon become callous to
the feel of their touch."

Exegete-preachers may come to the point where they have analyzed the verses and read the literature so carefully, that their
hearts are no longer stirred. They know the Fourth Gospel so well
that it has become a preaching tool instead of a voice in which God
is speaking *to us*. How often I have listened to a sermon and, rather
than discovering blessing, found myself *reconstructing my own sermon based on the same text!* Rather than hearing a fresh word from
God, I was planning what I would teach or preach someday.

I have come to evaluate commentaries by what I call "depth exegesis." I value a commentary whose author has been personally touched by the power of the text. There is genuine spiritual insight in such works, not just the recital of scholarly facts. Take a careful look at a typically technical volume on John and compare it with *The Fourth Gospel* by Edwin C. Hoskyns and F. N. Davey.[2] Most march though the interpretative details of the text, while Hoskyns and Davey draw spiritual insights into each discussion. William Temple's 1945 work[3] does the same, as does J. E. Lesslie Newbigen's more recent exposition.[4]

What makes these books different? *The authors move from within the thought of the Gospel.* Moreover, their own lives have been affected by what they have read.

At my desk before the open text of John I often look at the commentaries and the critical Greek edition with its many notes—and pray. I ask that in some fashion God will speak to me *first*, and only then will my own fresh, invigorating experience with the passage empower the message. A friend has a name for sermons that seem lifeless because the preacher stands apart from the power of the story. Such work, she says, is "doing theology from the outside." Such empty spirituality accomplishes nothing but lifeless ritual.[5]

Sermons graced by prayer and spiritual hunger take on a tangible vitality. Hearers sense an authenticity and compelling truth they cannot neglect because the preacher speaks of truths personally experienced.

A Preaching Cycle Through John

Everyone should take the time to personally examine the text of John, seeing for themselves the native literary divisions. Yet students often ask for guidance in organizing the Gospel into topical

2. London: Faber and Faber, 1947.
3. *Readings in St. John's Gospel*, 1st and 2d series (London: Macmillan, 1945).
4. *The Light Has Come: An Exposition of the Fourth Gospel* (Grand Rapids: Eerdmans, 1982).
5. The most powerful description of this dangerous phenomenon is given in Karl Barth's commentary on Romans. In his remarks on Romans 2, Barth compares us with people who live on the edge of an empty canal. The channel was designed to carry water, has the marks of water inside, and even holds the promise of one day providing water. But we grow accustomed to the canal's emptiness *because it has been so long since any water flowed.*

units. The literary analysis offered in chapter 5 offers a splendid place to begin.

The very best thing is to enjoy the Fourth Gospel personally. Make its text—complete with its interpretative challenges—a place of nourishment and spiritual stimulation. *Live in the Gospel of John for nine months and you and your congregation will be richly rewarded.* Nine months of preaching (thirty-nine messages) would cover the entire text in the program suggested below. However John is used, the exegete should, above all, learn to have fun and to communicate the sheer enjoyment of each pericope. The insights, the drama, the surprises, and the inspiration John provides are without parallel elsewhere in the New Testament.

Preaching through the Gospel of John

1:1–18	The incarnation and the glory of the Word
1:19–34	The baptism and anointing of Jesus
1:35–51	Discipleship
2:1–12	The messianic wedding at Cana
2:13–25	Jesus and the Jerusalem temple
3:1–21	Jesus, Nicodemus, and being "born again"
3:22–36	Jesus and John the Baptist
4:1–54	Jesus in Samaria and Cana of Galilee
5:1–47	Jesus' authority
6:1–34	The feeding of the five thousand
6:35–71	Bread from heaven and communion
7:1–39	Jesus at the Feast of Tabernacles
7:40–52	How Jesus divides an audience
7:53–8:11	The woman caught in adultery[6]
8:12–59	The true identity of Jesus and his followers
9:1–41	Being blind and gaining sight
10:1–21	Jesus the good shepherd
10:22–42	Jesus and the Feast of Hannukah
11:1–44	The story of Lazarus: A model of death and life
11:45–57	The plot to kill Jesus
12:1–19	The anointing and triumphal entry of Jesus
12:20–50	Why some people are curious and some believe
13:1–20	Jesus washes the disciple's feet
13:21–38	Betrayal and glorification

---

6. While this story has a problematic textual history, it bears all of the marks of being an authentic story from Jesus. It is a truly beloved passage.

Appendix

A Bibliography of Commentaries

There seems to be no end to the commentaries that are published year after year on the Fourth Gospel. A quick glance at the commentary section in a theological library shows that the Johannine writings receive more than their fair share of attention. This proliferation of publishing interest has gone on for years. This means that, as we look for volumes that comment on the message of John, we have to use judgement so that we reach for the best books. Not just any commentary will do. Rather, volumes have to be selected for the project at hand, whether it be an exegetical analysis of the Greek text, a sermon, or pastoral homilies for chapel talks.

The following list includes commentaries that appear most frequently in the library. The symbols I have given will serve as a key to indicate the use of John's Greek text and the volumes' relative usefulness for exegesis. This is my personal evaluation and in no way should be deemed absolute. As with music, preference of commentaries is a personal matter!

I look for commentaries that balance discussion of "critical issues" with genuine creative insight. Some commentaries seem to do nothing more than advance a theological argument lifted from the pages of the technical journals. Others give pastoral insights but fail to reap the benefits of modern research.

It is especially difficult to advise students about which commentaries they should select among the books they purchase for lifetime use. But there is no doubt that the most "worn" volumes on my shelves are those written by Raymond E. Brown, C. K. Barrett, George R. Beasley-Murray, Edwin C. Hoskyns and F. N. Davey, Barnabas Lindars, Leon Morris, and Rudolf Schnackenburg. Among these seven, Brown tops the list.

Therefore, the following bibliography is evaluated according to my own system. Symbols (▲) indicate level of expertise needed to understand the author's use of Greek.

▲▲ Exhaustive use of the Greek text. Sometimes difficult for students who do not use Greek.

▲ Substantial use of the Greek, but accessible to students who do not use Greek. The text consistently provides an English translation of the passage under discussion.

Boxes (❑) indicate the depth and thoroughness and general merit of the work:

❑❑❑❑ One of the best commentaries. An essential resource for all exegetical studies.

❑❑❑ An excellent commentary which frequently provides excellent insights.

❑❑ One of the better commentaries which, while not lengthy and thorough, still is quite useful and creative in exegesis.

❑ A minor commentary which, though not well known, still should not be overlooked because of its brevity, age, or style.

Barclay, William. *The Gospel of John*, 2 vols. Edinburgh, Scotland: St. Andrew's, 1956; various North American eds. ❑
Barrett, C. K. *The Gospel According to St. John: An Introduction with Commentary and Notes on the Gospel Text*, 2d ed. Philadelphia: Westminster, 1978. ▲▲❑❑❑❑
____. "John," in Matthew Black and H. H. Rowley, eds., *Peake's Commentary on the Bible*. New York: Nelson, 1962, 844–69. ❑❑

Beasley-Murray, George R. *John*. In *Word Biblical Commentaries*. Waco, Tex.: Word, 1987. ▲▲☐☐☐☐

Bernard, John Henry. *Critical and Exegetical Commentary on the Gospel of St. John*, 2 vols. A. H. McNeile, ed. *International Critical Commentaries*. Edinburgh: T and T Clark, 1928. ▲▲☐☐☐

Blank, Josef. *New Testament for Spiritual Reading: The Gospel According to John*, vols. 2, 3 (vol. 1. by John J. Huckle and Paul Visokay). John L. McKenzie, gen. ed. New York: Crossroad, 1978–1981. ☐☐

Boice, James M. *The Gospel of John: An Expositional Commentary*. Grand Rapids: Zondervan, 1979. ☐

Brown, Raymond E. *The Gospel According to John*, 2 vols. In *Anchor Bible Commentaries*, New York: Doubleday, 1966–1970. ▲☐☐☐☐

Bruce, F. F. *The Gospel of John*. Grand Rapids: Eerdmans, 1983. ▲☐☐☐

Bultmann, Rudolf. *The Gospel According to John: A Commentary*, trans. George R. Beasley-Murray, ed. by R. W. N. Hoare and J. K. Riches. Philadelphia: Westminster, 1971. ▲▲☐☐☐

Burge, Gary M. "John." In *Evangelical Commentary on the Bible*, W. A. Elwell, ed. Grand Rapids: Baker, 1989, 840–80.

Carson, D. A. *The Gospel According to John*. Grand Rapids: Eerdmans, 1991. ▲☐☐☐

Dodd, C. H. *The Interpretation of the Fourth Gospel*. Cambridge, England: Cambridge University Press, 1953. ▲☐☐☐☐

Dodds, M. "The Gospel According to St. John." In *Expositor's Greek New Testament*, W. Robertson, Nicoll, ed., vol. 5. Grand Rapids: Eerdmans, 1952. ▲▲☐

Fenton, John C. *The Gospel According to St. John in the Revised Standard Version*. Oxford, England: Clarendon, 1970.

Filson, Floyd V. *The Gospel of St. John*. Atlanta: John Knox: 1963.

Haenchen, Ernst. *A Commentary on the Gospel of John*, 2 vols., trans. by R. W. Funk. In *Hermeneia Commentaries*. Philadelphia: Fortress, 1984. ▲▲☐☐☐

Hendriksen, William. *The Gospel of John*, 2 vols. In *New Testament Commentaries*. Grand Rapids: Baker, 1954. ▲☐☐

Hoskyns, Edwin C., and F. N. Davey. *The Fourth Gospel*. London: Faber and Faber, 1947. ▲☐☐☐☐

Howard, Wilbert F. "Introduction and Exegesis," *The Gospel According to St. John*. In *The Interpreter's Bible*, George A. Buttrick, gen. ed., vol 8. Nashville: Abingdon, 1952.

Huckle, John J., and Paul Visokay. *New Testament for Spiritual Reading: The Gospel According to John*, vol. 1 (vols. 2, 3 by Josef Blank). John L. McKenzie, gen. ed. New York: Crossroad, 1978–1981. ☐☐

Hull, W. E. *John*. In *Broadman Bible Commentaries*, Clifton J. Allen, gen. ed., vol. 9. Nashville: Broadman, 1970.

Hunter, Archibald M. *According to John: The New Look at the Fourth Gospel.* Philadelphia: Westminster, 1968. ❐

Kealy, Sean P. *That You May Believe: The Gospel According to St. John.* St. Paul: Middlegreen, Slough, 1978.

Kysar, Robert. *John's Story of Jesus.* Philadelphia: Fortress, 1984. ❐

_____. *John.* In *Augsburg Commentaries on the New Testament.* Minneapolis: Augsburg, 1986. ❐❐

Lightfoot, Robert H. *St. John's Gospel.* Oxford, England: Oxford University Press, 1960. ❐

Lindars, Barnabas. *The Gospel of John.* In *New Century Commentaries.* London: Oliphants, 1972.▲❐❐❐

MacGregor, G. H. C. *The Gospel of John.* Garden City, N.Y.: Doubleday, Doran, 1928.

McPolin, J. *John.* Dublin, Ireland: Veritas, 1979.

MacRae, George W. *Invitation to John: A Commentary on the Gospel of John with Complete Text from the Jerusalem Bible.* New York: Doubleday, 1978.

Marsh, John. *The Gospel of Saint John.* In *Penguin Commentaries.* Philadelphia: Westminster, 1968. ▲❐

Morris, Leon. *The Gospel of John.* In *New International Commentaries.* Grand Rapids: Eerdmans, 1970. ▲❐❐❐

Newbigin, J. Lesslie. *The Light Has Come: An Exposition of the Fourth Gospel.* Grand Rapids: Eerdmans, 1982. ❐❐❐

Plummer, Alfred. *The Gospel According to St. John.* In *Thornapple Commentaries.* Grand Rapids: Baker, 1981. ▲

Richardson, A. *The Gospel According to St. John.* In *Torch Bible Commentaries.* New York: Macmillan, 1960.

Sanders, Joseph N., and B. A. Mastin. *A Commentary on the Gospel According to St. John.* In *Harper Commentaries.* London: A. and C. Black, 1968. ▲❐❐

Schnackenburg, Rudolf. *The Gospel According to St. John,* 3 vols., trans. K. Smith. New York: Seabury, 1979. ▲❐❐❐❐

Sloyan, Gerald S. *John.* In *Interpretation Commentaries.* Atlanta: John Knox, 1988. ❐❐

Smith, D. Moody. *John.* Philadelphia: Fortress, 1976. ❐❐

Strachan, Robert H. *The Fourth Gospel.* London: SCM, 1941.

Tasker, Randolph V. G. *The Gospel According to St. John: An Introduction and Commentary.* In *Tyndale Commentaries.* Grand Rapids: Eerdmans, 1960. ❐

Temple, William. *Readings in St. John's Gospel.* London: Macmillan, 1945. ❐❐

Tenney, Merrill C. *John: The Gospel of Belief.* Grand Rapids: Eerdmans, 1948

_____. *The Gospel of John.* In *The Expositor's Bible Commentary,* vol 9, Frank E. Gaebelein, ed. Grand Rapids: Zondervan, 1981. ❐❐

Vawter, Bruce. "The Gospel According to John." In *The Jerome Biblical Commentary*, Raymond E. Brown, Joseph A. Fitzmyer, and Roland E. Murphy, eds. Englewood Cliffs, N.J.: Prentice-Hall, 1968: 414–66. ◻

Westcott, Brooke Foss. *Commentary on the Gospel According to St. John*. 1889. Repr. ed. Grand Rapids: Eerdmans, 1973. ▲◻◻

_____. *The Gospel According to St. John: The Greek Text with Introduction and Notes*. 1908. Repr. ed., Grand Rapids: Baker, 1980. ▲▲◻◻